D1196330

"*Character Carved in Stone* vividly captures many of the life lessons I learned as a student and athlete at West Point. You'll find it well worthwhile to live in these stories and learn these principles! In his latest book, Pat Williams shows you, step by step, just how you can acquire the leadership skills and character traits that are the foundation of the United States Military Academy. This book is a difference maker!"

Brig. Gen. Pete Dawkins, US Army (Ret); distinguished graduate, US Military Academy at West Point, 2002

"The world needs leaders with strong character more than ever. Pat Williams's book on the twelve leadership values at West Point is right on target. These values have stood the test of time and produced some of this country's most outstanding leaders. This book is a must-read if we want people who can solve the big challenges we all face."

Gen. Richard B. Myers, US Air Force (Ret); 15th chairman, Joint Chiefs of Staff; president, Kansas State University

"Pat has written a splendid book about the virtues that define a West Point education and differentiate it from all other universities. I enjoyed his book and heartily recommend it."

Col. Frank Borman, US Air Force (Ret); commander, Apollo 8

"I love the fact that Pat Williams has taken the twelve core virtues of West Point and created this new and exciting book. I was taught those virtues and have used them in everything that I have done since my graduation."

Mike Krzyzewski, head men's basketball coach, Duke University

"Pat Williams has done a masterful job of reminding us that leaders are made—not born. *Character Carved in Stone* reminds me of the DNA of greatness as evidenced in the pages of this great read."

Gen. Tommy R. Franks, US Army (Ret); former commander in chief, United States Central Command

"Character used to mean something other than a funny person. Pat Williams reminds us of what true character looks like and where to find it."

Cal Thomas, syndicated columnist

"If you're looking for a great inspirational read with an American military history theme, look no further. In *Character Carved in Stone*, Pat Williams matches up the twelve leadership virtues of

West Point with true stories from academy-trained heroes—every chapter is a lesson in character qualities expected of military officers. I have often said the world is in desperate need of a new leadership role model. Readers who apply these time-tested principles to their lives and work will be well on their way to fulfilling that need."

Ken Blanchard, coauthor, *The New One Minute Manager* and *Servant Leadership in Action*

"Every time I scouted a game at Army West Point my spirits were lifted sky high. I had the same reaction while going through *Character Carved in Stone*. Get ready for a memorable reading experience."

Ernie Accorsi, former general manager, New York Giants

"Today's leaders are hungry for the wisdom and inspiration they will find in Pat Williams's new book, *Character Carved in Stone*. His stories and principles will enable readers to apply his vision to their leadership lives today. West Point's first classes began inspiring the young men of our county in 1802 and its twelve core values continue to do so for our young men and women. *Character Carved in Stone* opens new doors for today's leaders."

Frances Hesselbein, chairman, the Frances Hesselbein Leadership Forum; former CEO, Girl Scouts of the USA; recipient, Presidential Medal of Freedom

"My character-building journey, which continues today, got a herculean jump with my four years as a cadet at West Point. As a career army officer, nothing contributed more to my success than being a leader of character based on the virtues described here. The marvelous stories that Pat captures bring to life powerful lessons that can be of value to any leader, in any business, at any level. You cannot possibly read this book and not feel compelled to raise the bar on how you lead—it is that good."

Brig. Gen. Jeffrey W. Foley, US Army (Ret); class of 1978, US Military Academy at West Point; coauthor, *Rules and Tools for Leaders*

"My time at West Point shaped me as an officer and as a leader, so I know it's a special place. Pat Williams's book *Character Carved in Stone* captures the essence and values of what I consider to be one of America's greatest leadership institutions. For anyone who wants to become the best leader they can be, I recommend you read this book immediately."

Matt Caldwell, president and CEO, Florida Panthers and Sunrise Sports & Entertainment

"By drawing vital leadership lessons from the grit, courage, and tenacity of United States Military Academy graduates such as Ulysses S. Grant, Dwight Eisenhower, Omar Bradley, Buzz Aldrin, and Norman Schwarzkopf, *Character Carved in Stone* reminds us why there's nothing better than West Pointers at their best. By spotlighting the virtues and values that propelled these Americans to greatness, Pat Williams's inspiring new book invites readers to join their ranks."

Robert M. S. McDonald, professor of history, US Military Academy at West Point; editor, *Thomas Jefferson's Military Academy: Founding West Point*

"I love West Point and I know Pat Williams does too. His new book captures the essence of these hallowed grounds in a very special manner. Read and be inspired."

Jeff Monken, head football coach, US Military Academy at West Point

"Pat Williams seamlessly blends memories of great American heroes all with Army West Point ingrained in them. He does a masterful job of showing the reader how impactful the United States Military Academy is in nurturing leaders of character . . . what a terrific read this is!"

Dave Magarity, head women's basketball coach, US Military Academy at West Point

"This book truly captures the essence of West Point and its incredible history. Not only does it tell wonderful stories about the graduates but it gives us a blueprint to help us improve many aspects of our lives. Thank you, Pat, for this tremendous book and the life lessons!"

Jimmy Allen, head men's basketball coach, US Military Academy at West Point

"In *Character Carved in Stone*, Pat Williams makes the rich traditions of West Point come alive. You won't be content to merely read this book. You'll want to live it. The stories will inspire you, the principles will empower you, and the wisdom in these pages will challenge you to carve your own character in stone."

Lt. Gen. Robert L. Caslen, Jr., US Army (Ret); 59th superintendent, US Military Academy at West Point

Also by Pat Williams and Jim Denney

Coach Wooden
Coach Wooden's Greatest Secret
The Difference You Make
The Sweet Spot for Success
Coach Wooden's Forgotten Teams

CHARACTER CARVED IN STONE

The 12 Core Virtues *of* West Point
That Build Leaders *and* Produce Success

PAT
WILLIAMS
with Jim Denney

Revell
a division of Baker Publishing Group
Grand Rapids, Michigan

© 2019 by Pat Williams and James Denney

Published by Revell
a division of Baker Publishing Group
PO Box 6287, Grand Rapids, MI 49516-6287
www.revellbooks.com

Printed in the United States of America

Library of Congress Cataloging-in-Publication Data
Names: Williams, Pat, 1940– author. | Denney, Jim, 1953– author.
Title: Character carved in stone : the 12 core virtues of West Point that build leaders and produce success / Pat Williams with Jim Denney.
Description: Grand Rapids, MI : Revell, a division of Baker Publishing Group, [2019]
Identifiers: LCCN 2018026758 | ISBN 9780800728830 (cloth)
Subjects: LCSH: Character—Religious aspects—Christianity. | Leadership—Religious aspects—Christianity. | United States Military Academy—Influence. | United States Military Academy—Alumni and alumnae.
Classification: LCC BV4599.5.C45 W54 2019 | DDC 241/.4—dc23
LC record available at https://lccn.loc.gov/2018026758

DISCLAIMER: The articles and other content which appear in this publication are unofficial expressions of opinion. The views expressed therein are those of the respective authors and do not reflect the official positions of the United States Military Academy, Department of the Army, or Department of Defense.

19 20 21 22 23 24 25   7 6 5 4 3 2

They say that if you have ever been to boot camp, you will never forget your drill sergeant. That's certainly true in my case. My drill instructor was Sergeant Enrique Fishbach. He was all soldier—posture like a pillar of granite, immaculate uniform, and shoes polished like mirrors. He had an impact on everyone who served under him at Fort Jackson, South Carolina, as I did for eight weeks of basic training in the fall of 1964.

I dedicate this book to Sergeant Fishbach with great respect.

I also dedicate this book to my father and mother, Jim and Ellen Williams, who daily instilled these principles in me when I was a youngster growing up in Wilmington, Delaware.

Contents

Foreword

THE BEST DECISION I NEVER MADE

*C*oach *Mike Krzyzewski was a point guard at Army from 1966 to 1969. He returned as Army's head basketball coach in 1975, then served as head men's basketball coach at Duke University from 1980 to the present. He has led the Duke Blue Devils to five NCAA Championships, twelve Final Fours, twelve ACC regular season titles, and fourteen ACC Tournament championships. He has coached the USA men's national basketball team to Olympic gold medals in 2008, 2012, and 2016, and is a two-time inductee of the Naismith Memorial Basketball Hall of Fame.*

‡—♦—♦†

As a high school basketball player, I was the leading scorer in the Catholic League in Chicago for two years, and an All-State player. I had scholarship offers from Division I schools, and I was leaning toward Creighton, or maybe Wisconsin.

Then twenty-five-year-old Coach Bob Knight of the United States Military Academy at West Point came to our family's apartment, hoping to persuade me to play for Army. I thought, *I'm not going to West Point! I don't want to carry a rifle! I want to dribble behind my back and throw fancy bounce passes!*

But while I was in the living room with Coach Knight, my mom and dad were in the kitchen, speaking Polish to each other—and speaking loudly enough that I could hear. They had never taught me the Polish language, so I couldn't understand everything they said, but they dropped in enough English words that I got the gist—words like *Mike* and *stupid*.

Here I was, a Polish kid from Chicago being offered a full ride to the school where presidents and war heroes and astronauts went—and my parents couldn't believe I was turning it down. My father was an elevator operator and my mom was a cleaning lady. Though they had limited education, my parents had enormous respect for education and for the limitless opportunities America offered. How could their kid be so dumb as to say no to the Academy?

So they talked me into it. I still didn't want to go, but I trusted them because I loved them. I said, "Okay, I'll go to West Point." It was the best decision I never made.

My four years at West Point became the foundation of everything I am right now. It was exciting to be on a great team with talented players, coached by Bob Knight, who was at the beginning of a legendary coaching career. We always had a winning record, and we went to the NIT, which in those days was as big as the NCAA. I became captain of the basketball team, which was a great leadership training experience.

My two key mentors at West Point were Coach Knight and Colonel Tom Rogers, my officer representative and counselor at the Academy. In 1969, during my senior year, my father died suddenly of a cerebral hemorrhage. He had always been my most important guide and role model. How would I make decisions about my life and career without my father to talk to? Yet Coach Knight and Colonel Rogers were there to listen, counsel, and provide the wisdom that my father could no longer give. Both men remained close to me, not only during my time of loss but over the years that followed.

After graduation, I served in the US Army from 1969 to 1974. I spent time in South Korea, stationed a few miles from the demilitarized zone. I also coached service teams and spent two years coaching at the US Military Academy Prep School at Belvoir, Virginia. After my discharge from the Army, I worked for one year as a graduate assistant to Coach Knight at Indiana University. I returned to West Point as head coach, serving from 1975 to 1980. It was largely at Colonel Rogers's urging that I pursued the head coaching position I now hold at Duke.

So I can truly say that West Point has shaped the course of my life. I wouldn't be where I am today if not for the Academy.

In this book, Pat Williams tells story after story of men and women who have upheld the highest traditions of the Academy. Through these stories, he shows us the values of the United States Military Academy in action. In these pages, he takes us on a tour of the history of the Long Gray Line—that vast corps of generations of West Point graduates, from the time the Academy was founded to the present day.

This book is organized around the twelve core virtues of West Point which have been carved into twelve granite benches near the Battle Memorial at Trophy Point above the Hudson River. Those benches weren't there when I was at West Point—they were placed there in 1984—but I know they offer a great place for a cadet to think, reflect, and pray while looking out over the river. Those benches would be a fine place to ponder an important decision, reflect on a troubling dilemma, or quietly thank God for good news from home. The virtues carved into those benches are a constant reminder of the qualities we need to live courageously and effectively in all circumstances.

The twelve West Point virtues that were carved into those granite benches have also been carved into the souls of the cadets of the Academy. Any man or woman who builds a life on the foundation of those twelve virtues will become, *by definition*, an ethical and effective leader whether in the military or in civilian life. These virtues will produce victory on the battlefield and in every other field of endeavor.

I've known Pat Williams for many years, and I can tell you that he embodies these twelve virtues in his own life. He has written one of those rare books that manages to entertain even as it motivates and inspires. It was a joy to read it, and it's a privilege to give it my hearty commendation.

Mike Krzyzewski
Head Men's Basketball Coach at Duke University
West Point Class of 1969
January 10, 2019

Acknowledgments

With deep appreciation I acknowledge the support and guidance of the following people who helped make this book possible:

Special thanks to Alex Martins, Dan DeVos, and Rich DeVos of the Orlando Magic.

Hats off to my associate Andrew Herdliska; my proofreader, Ken Hussar; and my ace typist, Fran Thomas.

Thanks also to my writing partner, Jim Denney, for his superb contributions in shaping this manuscript.

Hearty thanks also go to Andrea Doering and the entire Baker-Revell team for their vision and insight, and for believing that we had something important to say in these pages.

And, finally, special thanks and appreciation go to my wife, Ruth, and to my wonderful and supportive family. They are truly the backbone of my life.

Introduction

THE VIEW FROM TROPHY POINT

The United States Military Academy at West Point is situated on the western bank of the Hudson River, some sixty miles north of New York City. The history of West Point would make a fascinating book. The Continental Army first occupied the site in January 1778. It is the oldest continuously operational army post in America. The garrison fortifications were designed by the Polish military engineer Tadeusz Kościuszko and constructed from 1778 to 1780.

The fort was known as Fort Arnold during the Revolutionary War and was named after its commander, General Benedict Arnold. The name Benedict Arnold is now synonymous with "traitor," yet few people know what his act of treason was. He had made a secret deal to surrender Fort Arnold—that is, West Point—to the British in exchange for money. After Benedict Arnold's treachery was exposed, the army renamed the fortifications Fort Clinton. It became the site of the Military Academy in 1802.

A few years ago, Boo Corrigan, the athletic director at the Academy, invited me to speak at the Academy. I went up on a

Sunday afternoon and spoke to 850 athletes, both men and women, who participated in twenty sports at West Point. I also spoke to a gathering of West Point coaches and had lunch with the cadets.

After lunch, a cadet gave me a tour of the campus. The highlight of my tour was Trophy Point—so called because it contains a display of captured artillery pieces around a commemorative marble column. That column, the Battle Memorial, is topped by a winged statue representing glory in battle. From Trophy Point, I looked out over the Hudson River and saw the site where George Washington was stationed for a while during the Revolutionary War and where American forces stretched a sixty-five-ton iron chain between the riverbanks to halt the British Navy.

Arranged along the walkways near the Battle Memorial are twelve benches carved from costly pink granite. Each bench is inscribed with a word representing one of the twelve leadership virtues of West Point:

compassion	integrity
courage	loyalty
dedication	perseverance
determination	responsibility
dignity	service
discipline	trust

Bench from West Point

The twelve benches remind the cadets that these are the twelve essential character qualities they *must* exemplify as military officers. These are the leadership traits that lead to victory and success. By instilling these traits in the West Point cadets, the Military Academy has produced a long line of leaders and winners.

These traits are not born in us. They do not just happen. They are virtues that must be acquired by continually strengthening our character. We become role models of these twelve virtues by consciously and continuously working on them and building them into our lives by the decisions we make, hour by hour, day after day. It is worth our while to examine these twelve qualities closely and to align our thoughts and words and actions with all twelve. The twelve benches were donated in 1984 by members of the class of 1934 in celebration of the golden anniversary of their graduation. The cost of the twelve benches was $25,000. The project was headed by Colonel Robert G. Finkenaur, a West Point graduate who also taught mathematics at the Academy (among his math pupils was a young David Petraeus). On the occasion of the fiftieth reunion of the class of 1934, Colonel Finkenaur told his classmates, "I can't even imagine that anyone else in the class has had a less colorful professional history than mine since graduation."[1] I would take issue with the colonel's humble words.

Born in St. Louis, Missouri, Robert Finkenaur received an appointment to West Point in 1930 and served in the artillery branch of the army. Though he was never in combat, he held key posts during World War II and the Korean War before retiring in 1959. He served in the army unit that launched the first two-stage rocket at White Sands, New Mexico (a precursor to the multistage rockets that launched astronauts to the moon). He was a planner of the Operation Fortitude "phantom invasion," a deception that led the Germans to expect an invasion at Calais on the Straits of Dover, helping to ensure the success of the D-Day landings in Normandy in June 1944.

Colonel Finkenaur also assisted Generalissimo Chiang Kai-shek in establishing the Republic of China Military Academy after the Communist takeover of the Chinese mainland. He also assisted General Anthony "Old Crock" McAuliffe after World War II (McAuliffe commanded the 101st Airborne Division in Bastogne during the Battle of the Bulge and famously delivered a one-word reply to a German demand for surrender: "Nuts!"). So I would say that Colonel Finkenaur definitely had a colorful career in the United States Army.

Finkenaur claimed to be the worst horseman at West Point. He said the Academy assigned him a "perfectly cylindrical horse."

No matter how tightly he cinched the girth strap of the saddle, it would rotate around the horse, leaving Finkenaur under the belly of the horse instead of riding on the horse's back. When Finkenaur took part in saber drills on horseback, his blade invariably stuck fast in the sawdust-bag target, causing him to be unhorsed.

A few years ago, a journalist wrote a book that was highly critical of West Point and the United States military during the Vietnam era. The author wrote about the twelve benches lining the footpath at Trophy Point. "Presented to the academy by the class of 1934," he wrote, "each bench had been inscribed with a different virtue: DIGNITY, DISCIPLINE, COURAGE, INTEGRITY, LOYALTY. The effect was almost quaint, an anachronism."[2] Is that true? Are the virtues of West Point quaint and anachronistic? Do ideas such as dignity, discipline, courage, integrity, and loyalty belong to another age? Are they no longer relevant to our world today?

In a tribute to Colonel Finkenaur, who died in 1991, his son, James F. Finkenaur, resoundingly answered that cynical claim, writing, "If the benches are an anachronism, they better start shutting the place down."[3] Well said. If the twelve West Point virtues don't apply in today's world, then they never did—and the Academy at West Point need not exist. These virtues are twelve of the most important subjects taught at West Point. General H. Norman Schwarzkopf Jr., one of the Academy's most illustrious graduates, once observed, "Leadership is a potent combination of strategy and character. But if you must be without one, be without the strategy."[4]

I believe these twelve virtues are crucial to leadership and success in this or any era. If you exemplify these twelve character traits, you will be a leader, because you will stand head and shoulders above most of your peers as a person worthy of being followed and emulated. If you exemplify these twelve qualities, you will be a success in any endeavor you put your mind to, because no one who is a role model of these qualities could ever be considered a failure. Wherever you lead, these twelve virtues will magnify your influence and propel you toward great service, great goals, great achievements, and great distinction.

In this book, I have profiled many West Point–trained heroes who have served our nation with honor and distinction, from the Civil War era to the War on Terror. These heroes all exemplify these twelve virtues and demonstrate for us how to acquire them and put them into practice. Turn the page with me, and let's explore these twelve traits together. Let's discover how we can impact the world and achieve great things when our character has been forever carved in stone.

—— 1 ——

COMPASSION

WARRIOR WITH A HEART

Ulysses S. Grant was a brilliant general and a compassionate president but a complete failure as a businessman. Before earning fame as a Civil War general, he tried farming, selling real estate, selling firewood on street corners, and tanning leather. After leaving the White House, he started a financial company and went bankrupt. In those days, retired presidents did not receive a pension, and Grant had forfeited his army pension to run for office.

Nearly bankrupt and worried about leaving his wife in poverty if he died, Grant began writing articles about Civil War experiences. They were published in the *Century Magazine*, which paid him $500 per article. The editor urged Grant to compile the articles into a book, so Grant began writing his memoirs.

In the summer of 1884, Grant began suffering from a sore throat. He refused to see a doctor at first, and the soreness grew steadily worse. Finally, in October, he went to a doctor, who diagnosed him with cancer of the throat. Destitute and terminally ill, Grant wondered if he would live to complete his memoirs. His friend, novelist Mark Twain, had recently founded a publishing house, and he offered to publish Grant's memoirs and pay him a 75 percent royalty on all books sold (the industry standard was 10 percent). With the help of his son Frederick, who did research and fact-checking, Grant completed the manuscript just a few days before his death in July 1885. *The Personal Memoirs of U. S. Grant* was published later that year and became a critical and popular success. Grant's wife, Julia, collected $450,000 in royalties (the equivalent of millions today). Grant, who failed at every business he tried, became a bestselling author after his death.

Grant is famed for his boldness and brilliance as a strategist, and rightly so. But his most distinctive leadership trait often goes unnoted by historians and biographers. In the next few pages, we will look closely at the central pillar of Grant's strength as a leader—his compassion—and we will see why this is such an important trait for us to emulate in our own leadership lives.

+◆◆◆+

Ulysses S. Grant was born in 1822 and graduated from the United States Military Academy at West Point in 1843. After serving in the Mexican-American War, he married Julia Dent, and they had four children. He retired from the army in 1854. Thirty-two years old, without any skills for civilian life, Grant struggled to keep himself and his family out of poverty. During a trip to New York City, he happened to run into an old friend from West Point, Simon Bolivar Buckner. Grant couldn't afford train fare home, so Buckner gave Grant the money he needed.

Grant's financial desperation didn't prevent him from demonstrating compassion to his fellow man. His slave-owning father-in-law once gave Ulysses and Julia the gift of a slave named William Jones. Though Grant desperately needed cash and could have sold Jones for more than $1,500, he freed the man instead.

When the Civil War began in 1861, Grant raised a company of volunteers in Illinois, and Governor Richard Yates granted him a militia commission. Within weeks, Grant was promoted to colonel, then brigadier general. In August 1861, Major General John C. Frémont placed Grant in charge of the campaign to wrest control of the upper Mississippi River from the Confederates. Grant took Paducah, Kentucky, without a fight, then led his forces to victory at Belmont, Missouri, and Fort Henry, Tennessee.

Commanding seven gunboats and twenty-one thousand foot soldiers, General Grant faced his next objective, Fort Donelson on the bluffs of the Cumberland River. The garrison bristled with seventeen heavy artillery pieces and was manned by more than seventeen thousand Confederate soldiers. Grant attacked on February 13, 1862.

Union gunboats traded fire with the Fort Donelson gun batteries. By the second day of battle, the Confederate artillery had forced the gunboats to retreat out of range. On the third day, the Confederates sent troops out of the fort to break the Union siege. By the end of the day, Grant's infantry had driven the Confederates back into the fort. The Confederates knew their situation was hopeless and made the decision to surrender.

The commander of Fort Donelson sent a staff officer through the lines with a white flag to seek a parley to discuss terms of surrender. The commander signed his name to the communiqué: Brigadier General Simon Bolivar Buckner—Grant's West Point classmate, the old friend who had given him train fare when he had been down and out in New York City.

After Grant read the communiqué from Buckner, he dictated a terse reply, stating, "No terms except an unconditional and immediate surrender can be accepted. I propose to move immediately upon your works."[1] When the story of Grant's demand was reported in the newspapers, Ulysses S. Grant was given a new nickname: "Unconditional Surrender Grant."

Grant's reply to his old friend seems harsh and lacking in compassion. But Grant could not afford to show leniency or compassion based on old favors and personal friendship. This was war, and war is a harsh business. Once Fort Donelson had capitulated, there would be a time and a place for compassion—but not until.

When Buckner received Grant's reply, he was shocked and angered. Buckner considered his old friend's response unduly harsh and punishing. He briefly considered withdrawing his offer of surrender—but what would that accomplish except more pointless deaths? Buckner replied that, due to the overwhelming odds, he would reluctantly "accept the ungenerous and unchivalrous terms which you propose."[2]

Grant ignored the accusatory tone of Buckner's message and issued orders: prepare to receive the Confederates' surrender. He repositioned his troops and strictly forbade any mistreatment of prisoners or pillaging of the nearby town of Dover. Though it was customary to force the vanquished commander to come to the victor's encampment in submission, General Grant went to General Buckner's headquarters to finalize the surrender.

Ulysses S. Grant was not some spit-and-polish martinet who insisted on military protocol. He was a practical, unpretentious leader, known for his informal manner (and sometimes criticized for his slouching, unmilitary posture and inattention to his uniform). He believed disputes were best settled face-to-face, and he saw no reason to further humiliate General Buckner. The Confederates had been humbled enough.

Taking only a few members of his staff and no bodyguards, Grant rode boldly to a tavern in Dover that served as the Confederate headquarters. It was a risky move. As he rode that Sunday morning, Grant saw hundreds of Rebel soldiers, weapons in hand, glaring in hatred. Any one of them could have ended his life at will.

Upon arriving, Grant learned that Buckner was only the temporary commander of Fort Donelson. The senior Confederate generals who had directed the battle, Generals John B. Floyd and Gideon Pillow, had escaped, leaving Buckner with the humiliating task of offering surrender. Grant later recalled, "In the course of our conversation, which was very friendly, he [Buckner] said to me that if he had been in command I would not have got up to Donelson as easily as I did. I told him that if he had been in command I should not have tried in the way I did."[3]

Neither man was eager to get down to the business of surrender. Grant avoided the subject by reminding his old friend about happier times at West Point. The two men reminisced for an hour, then Buckner sighed and said they should discuss the matters they had come to talk about.

General Grant assured General Buckner there would be no formal ceremony of Buckner surrendering his sword to Grant, no unnecessary humiliation. The two sides would cease hostilities, and the Confederates would bury their dead and go to prison for the duration.

Then Grant took Buckner aside and offered a gesture of friendship. "You may be going among strangers," Grant said, "and I hope you will allow me to share my purse with you."[4] Grant knew that, as a prisoner of war, Buckner would have major legal expenses. Buckner had joined the Confederate army while his home state, Kentucky, had remained in the Union. He could be tried for bearing arms against the United States. According to Grant's memoirs, General Buckner thanked him for his offer. (In a 1904 interview, Buckner remembered the incident differently, claiming he knocked the money purse from Grant's hands and walked away.)

General Grant's offer of financial aid to his defeated foe was an act of genuine compassion. Even in war, Grant didn't forget kindness and personal friendship. Yet his compassion did not erase his sense of duty. He took charge of his old West Point classmate and the other Confederate officers and sent them to the stockade at Fort Warren, Massachusetts.

Though Grant had gone to Buckner to open the surrender talks, Grant had Buckner come to him the following day to resolve all remaining questions. They met aboard the river steamer *New Uncle Sam*, Grant's floating headquarters. Though Grant had initially demanded "unconditional surrender" from the Confederates, by the time negotiations were concluded, he had made many compassionate concessions. Ulysses S. Grant was a ruthless warrior on the battlefield, but he became known as the "Compassionate Conqueror" at the negotiating table. Grant compassionately distributed Union rations to the underfed Confederate prisoners. He compassionately allowed the defeated officers to keep their swords, which were not only weapons but also symbols of rank and authority. He compassionately sent wounded prisoners to Union hospitals for treatment, and he allowed prisoners to send letters to their families.

When one of Grant's officers asked when the Rebels would be forced to stack their weapons and lower their flag, Grant replied that there would be no such ceremony. "The surrender is a fact. We have the fort, the men, and the guns. Why should we go through with vain forms and mortify and injure the spirit of brave men who, after all, are our own countrymen and brothers?"[5]

Lieutenant Colonel (later General) Horace Porter served as a staff officer to General Grant during the Civil War. As personal secretary to Grant during his presidency, Porter wrote one of the first biographies of Grant, *Campaigning with Grant*, published in 1897. He quoted General James Longstreet, Robert E. Lee's second in command, as praising Grant for his compassion. "General Grant had come to be known as an all-round fighter seldom, if ever, surpassed," said General Longstreet, "but the biggest part of him was his heart."[6]

Porter told stories about the compassionate heart of Ulysses S. Grant. He saw Grant get angry on only a single occasion, and that anger came straight from his compassion. Grant was a horseman, an animal lover, and a devout Christian who would not allow profanity in his presence. On one occasion, he and his officers rode at the head of the column of soldiers. Coming around a bend in the road, they came upon a civilian whose wagon was stuck in a mud pit in the road. The man was beating his horses in their faces with the hand grip of his whip while swearing a blue streak.

Grant spurred his horse forward and reached the man in moments. He dismounted and dashed to the man with his fists clenched, shouting, "Stop beating those horses!"

The man sneered at Grant and aimed another blow at the nearest horse. "Who's driving this team," he said, "you or me?"

"I'll show you," Grant said. Then he turned to one of his officers who had just ridden up. "Take this man in charge. Have him tied up to a tree for six hours as punishment for his brutality."

Porter recorded that General Grant's forces engaged in battle with the Confederates later that day. Yet his compassion for those abused horses was so great that, even during the fighting, he twice made vivid, angry remarks about that scoundrel who had beaten those horses. "This was the one exhibition of temper manifested by him during the entire campaign," Porter concluded, "and the only one I ever witnessed during my many years of service with him."[7]

General Grant's compassion was also evident in his aversion to the sight of blood and suffering. This seems paradoxical, since Grant undoubtedly witnessed a great deal of blood during the Civil War. Porter recorded that Grant "was visibly affected by his proximity to the wounded, and especially by the sight of blood. He would turn his face away from such scenes, and show by the expression of his countenance, and sometimes by a pause in his conversation, that he felt most keenly the painful spectacle presented by the field of battle."

Porter recorded one conversation he had with General Grant in which the general said, "I cannot bear the sight of suffering. The night before the first day's fight at Shiloh, I was sitting on the ground, leaning against a tree, trying to get some sleep. It soon began to rain so hard that I went into a log-house nearby to seek shelter; but I found the surgeons had taken possession of it, and were amputating the arms and legs of the wounded, and blood was flowing in streams. I could not endure such a scene, and was glad to return to the tree outside, and sit there till morning in the storm."[8]

Porter recorded another revealing glimpse into Grant's compassionate soul during one of the most brutal assaults of the Civil War, the Attack on the Bloody Angle (part of the Battle of Spotsylvania Court House). As aides galloped into Grant's camp with report after report of success on the battlefield, staff officers shouted and cheered, but Grant sat unmoving in his camp chair by the fire. Porter wrote:

[Grant] made very few comments . . . until the reports came in regarding the prisoners. When the large numbers captured were announced, he said, with the first trace of animation he had shown: "That's the kind of news I like to hear. I had hoped that a bold dash at daylight would secure a large number of prisoners." . . . His extreme fondness for taking prisoners was manifested in every battle he fought. When word was brought to him of a success on any part of the line, his first and most eager question was always, "Have any prisoners been taken?" . . . [This] was no doubt chiefly due to his tenderness of heart, which prompted him to feel that it is always more humane to reduce the enemy strength by captures than by slaughter. His desire in this respect was amply gratified, for during the war it fell to his lot to capture a larger number of prisoners than any general of modern times.[9]

President Abraham Lincoln admired General Grant—not so much for his compassion but for his relentless pursuit of victory.

Grant became a controversial figure during the war. His critics claimed he was a poor strategist who nearly lost the Battle of Shiloh. One of those critics was Alexander McClure, a Pennsylvania state politician and a supporter (and later, biographer) of President Lincoln. McClure recorded that he pleaded with Lincoln to fire General Grant:

> I appealed to Lincoln for his own sake to remove Grant at once. . . . I could form no judgment during the conversation as to what effect my arguments had upon him beyond the fact that he was greatly distressed at this new complication. When I had said everything that could be said from my standpoint, we lapsed into silence. Lincoln remained silent for what seemed a very long time. He then gathered himself up in his chair and said in a tone of earnestness that I shall never forget: "*I can't spare this man; he fights.*" That was all he said, but I knew that it was enough, and that Grant was safe in Lincoln's hands against his countless hosts of enemies.[10]

Compassion is not incompatible with leadership or with the conduct of war. In fact, the most compassionate leaders often make the most effective warriors, because they are driven by a compassionate desire to bring war to a swift, decisive, and merciful end. The Civil War dragged on inconclusively for far too long because President Lincoln's generals (such as Irvin McDowell and George B. McClellan) were overly cautious and wouldn't fight. Grant fought. Lincoln needed a general who would fight, so he refused to let Grant go.

◆◆◆

Grant fought hard to win the war—and he fought equally hard to win the peace. When accepting the surrender of Robert E. Lee at Appomattox Court House on April 9, 1865, Grant offered generous terms. He paroled Confederate prisoners, allowed soldiers to return to their homes, and permitted them to keep their horses and mules. Grant believed compassion was essential to winning the peace. He was infuriated when a federal grand jury charged Lee and other Confederate leaders with treason, violating the peace agreement he had negotiated.

After the assassination of Lincoln, Grant went to the White House and told President Andrew Johnson he would resign as commander of the army if the indictments against Lee and the other Confederate officers were not quashed. Grant was a wildly popular hero throughout the Union, and Johnson didn't dare to lose him, so he ordered the cases against the Confederates dropped.

President Andrew Johnson was the wrong man to implement Lincoln's dream of reuniting the Union, reconstructing the vanquished South, and guaranteeing the full citizenship of former slaves. Johnson battled the antislavery congressional Republicans and the Lincoln appointees in his cabinet. When Johnson vetoed the Civil Rights Act of 1866, Congress passed it over his veto.

In 1867, Congress passed the first of three Reconstruction Acts plus the Command of the Army Act, which placed Grant in charge of Reconstruction and required Johnson to pass any orders through Grant. Johnson tried to get Grant out of his way by suspending Secretary of War Edwin Stanton and appointing Grant as acting secretary of war. Johnson was maneuvering to get rid of both Stanton and Grant, but Grant outmaneuvered Johnson by accepting the job, then (after the Senate voted to reinstate Stanton) resigning before Johnson could appoint a replacement. These maneuverings enabled Grant and Stanton to carry out the will of the antislavery, pro–civil rights Congress over the objections of President Johnson.

Johnson's controversial attempt to thwart the will of Congress and suppress the rights of black Americans led to his impeachment. He escaped being removed from office by a single vote in the Senate. General Grant became an even more popular hero for standing up to Johnson. He became known as a leader who wanted to build on the compassionate legacy of Abraham Lincoln. Grant ran for president on the slogan "Let us have peace," and the nation elected him the eighteenth president of the United States. He served two terms, from 1869 to 1877.

Some historians have labeled Grant a successful Civil War general who was unsuccessful as president. But I think Grant succeeded on his own terms as a president of compassion. As a general, Grant successfully fought Andrew Johnson's attempts to undermine Abraham Lincoln's compassionate Reconstruction plan. As president, Grant led the Republican effort to protect African American civil rights while eradicating the last remnants of old Confederate nationalism and segregation.

Grant took an especially hard line against the Ku Klux Klan, which arose just after the fall of the South, spreading murder and terror against black Americans. As president, Grant sent his Justice Department to war against the Klan, securing thousands of indictments against leaders of the secret group. He promoted passage of the Ku Klux Klan Act in 1871, which empowered him to declare martial law and suspend habeas corpus wherever the Klan threatened an insurrection. Under that law, President Grant sent troops into South Carolina and brought many Klansmen to justice or sent them scurrying out of the state. Grant ultimately sent the Klan into hiding for years, and the hate group would not reemerge until the early twentieth century.

The goal of freedom for all Americans would not be completed in a single presidency—or a single century—but Lincoln and Grant did more to advance the cause of civil rights in America than any other leaders until Dr. Martin Luther King Jr.

Grant's presidency was marred by two scandals, the Gold Ring scandal of 1869 (a plot by financiers Jay Gould and Jim Fisk to dupe Grant into helping them corner the gold market; Grant foiled their scheme and prevented an economic depression) and the Crédit Mobilier bribery scandal involving his two vice presidents (first-term VP Schuyler Colfax and second-term VP Henry Wilson; Grant himself was innocent of wrongdoing). Grant tried mightily but unsuccessfully to alleviate the economic depression following the Panic of 1873.

Grant's presidency was enormously successful in terms of establishing justice, peace, and freedom for *all* citizens in the wake of a devastating Civil War and the legacy of slavery and injustice. The success of Grant's compassionate policies is reflected in the support he received from prominent abolitionists, civil rights leaders, and tribal leaders of the Native American nations. Frederick Douglass, the great African American social reformer, put it well:

> My confidence in General Grant was not entirely due to the brilliant military successes achieved by him, but there was a moral as well as military basis for my faith in him. He had shown his single-mindedness and superiority to popular prejudice by his prompt cooperation with President Lincoln in his policy of employing colored troops, and his order commanding his soldiers to treat such troops with due respect. In this way he proved himself to be not only a wise general, but a great man.[11]

Ulysses S. Grant was one of only two West Point graduates to occupy the Oval Office (the other was Dwight D. Eisenhower). Though history handed him a nearly impossible challenge as president in the post–Civil War era, he answered the challenge forcefully and compassionately. Ulysses S. Grant, class of 1843, exemplified the finest traditions of the United States Military Academy at West Point. He was an authentic role model of compassion.

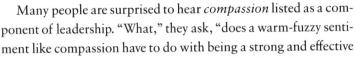

Many people are surprised to hear *compassion* listed as a component of leadership. "What," they ask, "does a warm-fuzzy sentiment like compassion have to do with being a strong and effective leader? In fact, doesn't compassion make a leader soft and weak? Shouldn't leaders want to be feared?"

During my fifty-plus years of serving in both the army and various professional sports organizations, I have gotten to know literally hundreds of leaders. I have always found that the most effective leaders have been people of great compassion. The compassionate leaders I have known were not necessarily feared, but they were always respected. They were tough when they had to be and compassionate when understanding was needed, but they were never "soft" or "weak."

I have also known leaders who thought of themselves as compassionate but did not know what compassion really is. They tried to lead by getting everybody to like them. They told people what would make them popular, not what needed to be said. If your so-called compassion comes from a desire to have everybody like you, you will be a weak leader. You will avoid controversy. You will back down when you need to stand firm. You will surrender when you should go to war. You will sugarcoat the hard truths, and you will confuse compassion with cowardice.

Leaders with authentic compassion are strong, courageous, honest, and direct. They say what needs to be said, but they say it with empathy and understanding. They are focused on what others need, not on making themselves look good. They set standards and hold people accountable for their own good and the good of the organization. Compassionate leaders will stand alone and stand firm to defend the defenseless and help the helpless. Compassionate leaders are a tyrant's worst nightmare.

What does a leader without compassion look like? Well, like Steve Jobs, the founder of Apple. Was Jobs successful? Amazingly so. He led Apple to the pinnacle of the tech world. His research and development teams produced some of the most admired products of our time: iPods, iPhones, iPads, MacBooks, and more. His vision reshaped our world. His company invented products we didn't even know we wanted—and once we saw them, we had to have them.

But Jobs had a dark side. He was seemingly devoid of compassion. As business journalist Ryan Tate observed, "Jobs regularly belittled people, swore at them, and pressured them until they reached their breaking point. In the pursuit of greatness, he cast aside politeness and empathy. His verbal abuse never stopped."[12] Malcolm Gladwell called Jobs "a bully," then listed his defects, all rooted in a lack of compassion for fellow human beings:

> Jobs gets his girlfriend pregnant, and then denies that the child is his. He parks in handicapped spaces. He screams at subordinates. He cries like a small child when he does not get his way. He gets stopped for driving a hundred miles an hour, honks angrily at the officer for taking too long to write up the ticket, and then resumes his journey at a hundred miles an hour. He sits in a restaurant and sends his food back three times. He arrives at his hotel suite in New York for press interviews and decides, at 10 PM, that the piano needs to be repositioned, the strawberries are inadequate, and the flowers are all wrong: he wanted calla lilies. (When his public-relations assistant returns, at midnight, with the right flowers, he tells her that her suit is "disgusting.")[13]

Okay, you might say, Jobs had a heart like a lump of coal—yet he was a billionaire, one of the most successful leaders in history. His lack of compassion didn't seem to hurt him.

Yet it did. Jobs's Grinch-hearted behavior is not the reason for his success. He succeeded because he was a visionary genius who had an uncanny ability to invent products the public would want. But the way he terrorized his subordinates actually caused him significant humiliation and sent some of his best talent fleeing to competitors.

Fortune's Adam Lashinsky tells how Jobs's lack of compassion harmed his company's reputation for quality. In 2008, Apple rolled out an iPhone internet-based system called MobileMe. It was a disaster, filled with bugs and malfunctioning features. Users hated it, and reviewers gave MobileMe a big black eye. Jobs called a meeting of the MobileMe tech team and proceeded to verbally abuse his people for a solid half hour. He used obscenities and personal insults to shame them, saying, "You've tarnished Apple's reputation. You should hate each other for having let each other down." In front of the group, he demoted the team leader and named a replacement.

An aberration? No. This incident, Lashinsky said, was typical of the "ruthless corporate culture" Jobs created at Apple—a culture that was often "brutal and unforgiving."[14]

Who was to blame for the embarrassing rollout of MobileMe? Steve Jobs. His terroristic management style created a corporate culture in which no one dared give him bad news. The MobileMe team didn't fail because of lack of talent or effort. They had worked feverishly, putting in long hours with little sleep in the hope of perfecting the system in time for the unveiling. When the team realized MobileMe would not be perfected on time, no one dared to tell Jobs. Leaders who rule by fear cut themselves off from vital information.

Our greatest leaders have always been people of compassion. Ulysses S. Grant, George Washington, Abraham Lincoln, Sojourner Truth, Susan B Anthony, Helen Keller, Martin Luther King Jr., Nelson Mandela, Mother Teresa, Ronald Reagan, and Malala Yousafzai altered the course of history while demonstrating kindness and respect for the people they led. The late UCLA head basketball coach John Wooden won ten NCAA national championships (including seven consecutive titles) and never swore at or demeaned his players. He was famed and beloved for his compassionate coaching style.

It is certainly possible to motivate people with fear, but love is a vastly more powerful motivator. When people feel safe around you, when they know they can take risks (and occasionally fail) and aren't afraid you will demote them, humiliate them, or destroy them in front of their peers, you will be amazed at what they can achieve. Love, trust, and loyalty encourage people to use their ingenuity and creativity to accomplish great things. Fear causes people to hide mistakes, play it safe, and even sabotage the leader and the organization.

Compassion builds trust and loyalty. When people know that you, the leader, genuinely care about them, they will go through walls for you. They will work extra-long hours and put forth an extra-intense effort—not because they fear you but because they love you, respect you, and want you to be proud of them.

To be a great leader, carve the virtue of compassion into the granite of your character. Be a leader like Ulysses S. Grant, whose indomitable will, fierce fighting spirit, and battlefield successes all began with a genuine love for his fellow human beings. Great warriors and great leaders are driven—first, last, and foremost—by hearts brimming with compassion.

2

COURAGE

MASTERY OVER FEAR

Alexander "Sandy" Ramsey Nininger Jr., West Point class of 1941, was born in Gainesville, Georgia, in 1918 and raised in Fort Lauderdale, Florida. One night when Nininger was five years old, he started climbing the stairs without turning on the light. His parents said, "Sandy, it's dark up there, aren't you afraid?"

"I'm not afraid," he said. "God is with me."

As a boy, Nininger hated the thought of killing any living creature. When his father shot a hawk near their home, Nininger argued with his dad, asking how he could be so cruel. Nininger's father explained that the hawk is a killer that preys on smaller birds. He didn't take any joy in killing, but he killed the hawk to protect the other birds.

Nininger wrestled with the idea of killing one creature to save many others. Finally, he decided that if necessary, he could kill— but he would *never* kill any creature or human being *except* to save innocent lives. After he graduated from West Point, he wrote to a friend that he felt no hatred toward any other person, nor would he ever be able to kill anyone out of hate.

Lean, tall, with corn-silk hair, Nininger was known to his friends and instructors as a quiet and studious young man. As head of the Lecture and Entertainment Committee at West Point, he went to New York and persuaded the producers and cast of the hit Broadway show *Arsenic and Old Lace* to give a performance at West Point.

During his time at the Academy, Nininger befriended an instructor, Colonel O. J. Gatchell, and his wife, and he enjoyed many Sunday afternoons in the Gatchells' home overlooking the Hudson. They would sit by the fire and have long conversations while listening to musical recordings. Nininger was a devotee of classical music, especially Tchaikovsky's Sixth Symphony. He could converse knowledgeably on a range of subjects, from music to history to Einstein's theory of relativity.

Nininger graduated from the United States Military Academy at West Point in May 1941, twenty-fourth in a class of 426. When he was commissioned as a second lieutenant in the infantry, he asked to be posted in the Philippines. During a brief furlough before being sent overseas, he called on Congressman Mark Wilcox, who had sponsored his appointment to the Academy. "Sandy," the congressman said, "why did you choose to be assigned to the Philippines?"

"Because," Nininger replied, "I feel that I can serve my country best over there."

He spent three days at home with his mother and father before shipping out. His mother told him she was worried for him. War raged in Europe, and she feared that the United States would soon be drawn into a global war—and he would be on the front lines.

Nininger hugged his mother and told her he had volunteered to serve his country. "Remember," he said, "you're the mother of a soldier."[1]

Lieutenant Nininger was posted to the Philippines with the First Battalion, Fifty-Seventh Infantry Regiment, Philippine Scouts. He had been in the Philippines for just a few weeks when Japan attacked Pearl Harbor on December 7, 1941, drawing the United States into World War II. The following day Japan attacked the Commonwealth of the Philippines, an American protectorate. Soon afterward, Japanese troops landed at major Philippine ports, then pushed inland, forcing the Americans to abandon Manila and retreat to the peninsula of Bataan for a last stand.

Nininger and his men worked around the clock, clearing vegetation from a mangrove swamp to create a line of fire against invaders. They also dug foxholes and built up a defensive dike. They slept only in catnaps and were constantly besieged by the jungle heat and malaria-ridden mosquitoes. Through it all, Nininger seemed buoyant and indefatigable.

The commander of the Fifty-Seventh, Colonel George S. Clarke, returned from an inspection of the fortifications and told an officer on his staff, "It's worth a trip to the dike just to watch Nininger. He's happy. Actually happy. The more trouble he has with food and ammunition, the more pep he shows. It's contagious. You should see the way he has those men working! It's as though Sandy had trained all his life for this hour."[2]

Japanese snipers infiltrated the area, taking up positions in trees, inflicting death and terror on the Americans and Filipinos alike. There was no battle line. The enemy seemed to be everywhere. During the day, every road and footpath was an ambush waiting to happen. At night, the enemy sowed fear, pounding drums, exploding firecrackers, and howling.

Major Fred J. Yeager, captain of Company A at that time, recalled that Nininger came to him and offered to lead a team to find out where the enemy had broken through the defensive line.

The ditch would give them cover as they entered Japanese-held territory. Yeager approved the risky plan. Nininger led the patrol, discovered the position and strength of the enemy, and reported back to Yeager. The Americans mounted a counterattack and re-established their defensive line.

Major Yeager later said that, without Nininger's daring patrol mission, "the entire Bataan campaign would have ended in January instead of three months later. These three months, I believe, saved Australia and enabled us to end the war many months before it otherwise would have."

Is that possible? Could the courage of one twenty-three-year-old lieutenant really have had that big an impact on the course of the war? Major Yeager thought so. Major Yeager added that Nininger "was the most fearless and most courageous officer or soldier I have ever seen."[3]

On January 10, 1942, Nininger approached Colonel Clarke and offered to hunt down enemy snipers at night. Clarke agreed to let him try. He couldn't figure out how Nininger did it. The colonel couldn't see any sign of snipers in the trees. Nininger would check those same trees and start firing, and enemy snipers would fall to the ground.

Two days later, on January 12, Japanese troops broke through the American perimeter. The regiment was in danger of being overrun. Lieutenant Nininger loaded himself down with grenades and ammunition belts, picked up a Garand rifle and a machine gun, and loped off toward the hottest part of the action. Japanese infiltrators hid in foxholes and treetops, unleashing a fury of hot lead upon the Americans. Nininger ran toward the enemy, shot a sniper out of a tree—and took a bullet in the leg. He bandaged the wound himself, then got up and kept going.

With a hailstorm of bullets all around him, he moved toward enemy foxholes, silencing one gun nest after another with grenades. Soldiers from K Company watched him crawl, run, and toss grenades, ignoring the withering enemy fire. They later counted twenty dead infiltrators, neutralized by Nininger. Inspired by the lieutenant's courage, his comrades followed him into the fray. In response, Japanese artillery barraged the battle sector. Nininger continued making his way among the explosions toward the enemy positions.

Nininger's fellow soldiers watched in amazement as he spent the last of his ammunition and continued on, armed with only his bayonet. More enemy soldiers fell dead at the point of his blade.

Then Lieutenant Nininger's comrades saw him take a bullet in the upper body. He dropped and rolled into a shell crater. A medic crawled up and fell into the hole beside him, opened his shirt, and bandaged the wound. Then the medic told Nininger to stay put. He would call for a corpsman to help him get out of the shell crater and back to safety. Nininger refused, left the medic in the shell crater, and kept moving toward the enemy.

Soldiers later recalled watching Nininger struggle out of the crater and run toward the action. They saw him take another bullet, this time in the shoulder. The impact turned him sideways, but he reoriented himself and willed himself onward. In front of him were a Japanese officer and two enlisted men. Apparently, they also were out of ammunition, because all three men faced Lieutenant Nininger armed with only bayonets. Nininger confronted the first soldier, knocked his bayonet aside, and thrust forward with his own. The enemy soldier fell screaming, mortally wounded. The second enemy soldier leaped forward, and Nininger bashed him to the ground. The officer came at him, and Nininger lunged with his bayonet, sinking the blade into his foe.

Then, spent from exhaustion and loss of blood, Nininger collapsed to the ground. Moments later, the mortally wounded enemy officer fell across Nininger's legs. When American corpsmen reached Nininger, they found him and all three enemy soldiers dead.

No one knows how many enemy soldiers Lieutenant Nininger dispatched that day, but every American on the battlefield testified that the lieutenant always went wherever the fighting was fiercest. He set an example of courage and showed his troops that the enemy wasn't invincible. Had Sandy Nininger not been on the battlefield that day, the Japanese forces probably would have defeated the Fifty-Seventh Infantry Regiment in a single day.

In a letter to Nininger's parents dated December 7, 1945, Major Fred J. Yeager wrote:

> *Your son's character was faultless. Never have I met anyone who could bear the hardships of war more cheerfully. Never have I encountered one whose attention to duty was greater, or whose performance of tasks assigned was better. . . . He wanted to be regarded above all other considerations, as a man fulfilling West Point's guiding motto: Duty, Honor, Country.*[4]

Heedless of his own safety, Nininger saved many American and Filipino lives that day. Those he saved had many trials and sufferings ahead of them, including the infamous Bataan death march and years of punishing conditions in Japanese prison camps. Many would perish—but many survived, thanks to Nininger's sacrifice.

General Douglas MacArthur later stated that Nininger's actions that day provided the precious time MacArthur needed to organize the defense of Manila Bay and Corregidor. Through his sacrifice, Lieutenant Nininger single-handedly changed the course of the war.

When Sandy Nininger first asked to be sent to the Philippines, he said he felt he could best serve his country there. It was as if he felt he had a divinely appointed mission to accomplish in the Philippine Islands.

Alexander "Sandy" Ramsey Nininger Jr. died on January 12, 1942, and was buried in Saint Dominic Parish Church Cemetery in Abucay, Bataan. On January 29, 1942, President Franklin D. Roosevelt bestowed on him the first Medal of Honor of World War II for "conspicuous gallantry and intrepidity above and beyond the call of duty."

Today, the first division of cadet barracks at the Academy at West Point is named in Sandy Nininger's honor. In 2006, the Association of Graduates of the United States Military Academy created the Alexander R. Nininger Award for Valor at Arms for West Point graduates who display conspicuous courage in combat and uphold the values and virtues of West Point.

There are many forms of courage. Let me suggest a few kinds of courage we need in our world today.

First, there is *physical courage*—bravery in the face of physical danger, pain, and death. That is the kind of incredible courage Sandy Nininger displayed. Physical courage is the willingness to risk life and limb for the sake of other people or for a righteous cause.

Second, there is *moral courage*—the unshakable commitment to do what is right, regardless of the personal cost, regardless of opposition and criticism, regardless of the risk of being abandoned or hated, regardless of disapproval or condemnation by other people. Moral courage is the commitment to stand utterly alone and friendless to do what is right.

Third, there is *emotional courage*—the willingness to endure heartache, sadness, loss, anxiety, fear, depression, and other forms of emotional pain. This is the courage to face your life, your problems, and your emotions without turning to "emotional anesthetics" such as alcohol, street drugs, opioids, gambling, promiscuity, pornography, and other self-destructive behaviors.

Please understand, a person suffering from clinical depression or anxiety should seek treatment for that medical condition; in fact, it takes great emotional courage to admit you need treatment and to reach out for help. But self-medicating and numbing your emotions with addictive substances and destructive behavior reflect emotional cowardice and weakness.

Fourth, there is *intellectual courage*—the willingness to seek the truth wherever it leads, even if the truth challenges or contradicts your cherished beliefs. Intellectual courage means trying to look at every question from all sides, not just through the lens of your biases or wishes. Intellectual courage means always telling the truth, even when there is a price to pay for your honesty.

Fifth, there is *spiritual courage*—the willingness to ask the deep questions about God, existence, meaning, death, and life after death. Many people spend their entire lives avoiding these questions, putting them off until some later date "when I have more time" or "when I'm old and closer to death." But all of life is preparation for death. We have been given this life so that we may prepare ourselves for the life to come.

If we demonstrate spiritual cowardice by avoiding these questions throughout our lives, a day will come when the answers will be demanded of us—and we will not be ready. Those who are spiritually courageous will reach the end of life well prepared to face death.

Courage is essential to leadership. You cannot lead other people toward a goal or an objective without an abundance of courage. You cannot withstand danger and adversity without courage. You cannot endure physical duress and emotional stress without courage. The United States Army and the United States Military Academy at West Point have always been training grounds for leadership and proving grounds for courage.

West Point cadets and graduates live by the West Point honor code and the West Point motto, "Duty, Honor, Country." As soldiers and leaders of character, West Point graduates demonstrate a level of character and courage that America can rely on. West Point can teach subjects such as mathematics, strategy, history, and more, but can an institution teach bravery? Is courage a learnable trait? I say, "Yes, absolutely."

How, then, can we learn to be more courageous? How can we learn to grow in our physical, moral, emotional, intellectual, and spiritual courage? Let me suggest five ways you can proactively, aggressively become a more courageous human being in every dimension of your life. These steps to greater courage are rooted in the West Point tradition.

1. *Become a more disciplined person.* West Point builds character through a synthesis of the traditions of ancient Athens and the traditions of ancient Sparta. The Greek city-states of Athens and Sparta were less than a hundred miles apart, yet they had very different sets of cultural values. Athens was concerned primarily with the educational, cultural, and philosophical growth of the individual. The highly militarized city-state of Sparta focused on developing military leaders who were physically disciplined and fit, skilled in the warrior arts, and intensely devoted to their honor.

West Point's focus on physical fitness and physical stamina is designed, in part, to build a warrior's courage. The greater your physical strength and endurance, the more confident you will be to take on any challenge—and confidence magnifies courage. Confidence produces clear thinking, effective decision making, greater optimism, and a stronger will to fight. A more disciplined warrior will be a more courageous warrior.

2. *Face your fears.* Honestly take stock of your fears. Ask yourself, "What am I afraid of?" Make a list of the top five fears that plague you and hold you back. Are you afraid of making a career move? Afraid of commitment? Afraid of flying? Afraid of public speaking? Afraid of failure? Afraid of rejection? Afraid of death? Write your fears on a sheet of paper or in a notebook or journal. Read through your list of fears, then ask yourself, "How can I conquer these fears?"

The cure for fear lies in doing the thing that makes you afraid. Instead of avoiding your fears, meet them head-on. Afraid of public speaking? Join Toastmasters or take a class in public speaking at your local community college. Afraid of commitment? Carefully consider what *really* scares you. Examine your fear rationally and then decide what you need to commit yourself to, based on facts, not fear.

Facing and embracing your fears is the best way to overcome them. The longer you avoid your fears, the bigger they grow. When fear chases you, the first step of courage is to turn and confront it. That first step is the hardest. After you face your first and toughest fear, it becomes easier to face the next one, and the next, and the next.

And that is how you build your courage—one step at a time. Keep making the choice to face your fears, day after day, week after week, and fear will lose its power over you.

3. *Practice demonstrating courage every day.* Take advantage of opportunities to stand alone for what you believe in, make difficult decisions without second-guessing yourself, take risks for the sake of other people and righteous causes. Most people go through their days taking the path of least resistance. To build courage, take the less traveled path, the path of *greater* resistance, the path that requires *more* courage. As the West Point Cadet Prayer reminds us, "Make us to choose the harder right instead of the easier wrong, and never to be content with a half-truth when the whole can be won."[5]

I am sure you have been in a social situation in which someone made a remark that was offensive to your values, your beliefs, your country, the military, or your faith. There are always people who will make such statements, expecting everyone to nod and agree. Instead of pretending to go along, demonstrate courage. Speak up. Defend your beliefs. Do so calmly, rationally, and politely but firmly. Let the people around you know what you stand for, what you believe in, what you care about. Be willing to take a lonely and courageous stand for your values and your faith.

Be willing to make unpopular decisions. Leadership is not a popularity contest. In fact, courageous leadership often leads to loneliness, rejection, opposition, and criticism. "A true leader," said General Douglas MacArthur, "has the confidence to stand alone, the courage to make tough decisions, and the compassion to listen to the needs of others. He does not set out to be a leader but becomes one by the equality of his actions and the integrity of his intent."[6]

I think you will find that as you practice becoming morally, emotionally, intellectually, and spiritually courageous, you will also grow in your physical courage. No one enjoys suffering. Nobody looks forward to pain. Though we should all look forward to life after death in the presence of the Lord, no one looks forward to the process of dying. Yet as we conquer our fear of what other people think and say about us, we will ultimately overcome our fear of what other people may do to us.

4. *Embrace uncertainty.* Disliking uncertainty is normal. Wanting your life neatly mapped out, with no problems or crises, is also normal, but life doesn't work that way. Life is made up of interruptions to deal with, problems to solve, crises to face. Instead of wishing you could spend your life relaxing on a beach in Tahiti, embrace uncertainty, lean into your challenges, tackle your problems with enthusiasm, and respond to crises with a sense of mission. Instead of wishing your life was problem free, thank God that he finds you worthy to be his agent of healing and helping others in an uncertain world. Be willing to risk everything, to throw yourself into the fray, to spend your life in a worthy cause.

Like you, I would like to be safe and secure. I wish I didn't have to worry about life's uncertainties. I wish I didn't have to think about the terrible things that happen in this world. But I know what it means to hear a doctor say, "You have cancer." I know what it means to answer the phone and hear a voice say, "I'm sorry to be the one to tell you this, but—"

This is an uncertain world. Terrible things happen. But it is also a world in which beautiful things happen. You cannot receive all the good this world has to offer unless you are willing to embrace life with its uncertainties.

5. *Replace fear with faith.* Doubt produces fear. Faith replaces fear with courage. The more complete your trust in God, the more

bold and courageous you will be. If you are truly convinced that God is with you, leading you, protecting you, and giving you the strength to complete your mission, you will have all the courage you need.

Three thousand years ago, a godless warrior named Goliath squared off against a young Jewish boy named David in the Valley of Elah. The story of David and Goliath is familiar to most people, but few people understand what it is really about. It is not a story about David's fearlessness or about the triumph of the underdog. It is a story about the power of faith to transform fear into courage.

When David the shepherd boy faced nine-foot-tall Goliath, he knew his strength was no match for Goliath's and that his leather sling and five smooth stones were no match for Goliath's armor, sword, and shield. Yet David was confident he would defeat his opponent. Why? David had courage *not* because he had confidence in himself but because he had faith in the power of God:

> David said to the Philistine, "You come against me with sword and spear and javelin, but I come against you in the name of the Lord Almighty, the God of the armies of Israel, whom you have defied. This day the Lord will deliver you into my hands, and I'll strike you down and cut off your head. This very day I will give the carcasses of the Philistine army to the birds and the wild animals, and the whole world will know that there is a God in Israel. All those gathered here will know that it is not by sword or spear that the Lord saves; for the battle is the Lord's, and he will give all of you into our hands." (1 Sam. 17:45–47)

Then David proceeded to make good on his promise. He loaded his sling with a single smooth stone, took aim, and let it fly. The stone struck Goliath in the forehead, and he fell dead. David had courage when he faced Goliath—and his courage was a by-product of his faith.

Where did the courage of twenty-three-year-old Lieutenant Nininger come from? The same place the courage of five-year-old

Sandy Nininger came from as he faced the dark: "I'm not afraid. God is with me." Faith replaces fear with courage.

General Douglas MacArthur offered one more word of counsel for finding faith and courage when we face a frightening challenge. In the most quoted speech ever delivered at West Point, General MacArthur said on May 12, 1962:

> *Duty, Honor, Country*—those three hallowed words reverently dictate what you ought to be, what you can be, what you will be. They are your rallying point to build courage when courage seems to fail, to regain faith when there seems to be little cause for faith, to create hope when hope becomes forlorn. . . . In my dreams I hear again the crash of guns, the rattle of musketry, the strange, mournful mutter of the battlefield. But in the evening of my memory always I come back to West Point. Always there echoes and re-echoes: *Duty, Honor, Country.*[7]

If you know your duty, if you guard your honor, if you love your country, if you hold on to your faith, then you can pursue any goal, face any challenge, confront any enemy. You can live honorably, faithfully, courageously—for duty, honor, country.

3

DEDICATION

WHAT HEROES ARE MADE OF

On July 20, 1969, thirty-nine-year-old Buzz Aldrin, West Point class of 1951, became one of the first two human beings to land on the moon. He was the second man, after crewmate Neil Armstrong, to set foot on the lunar surface.

On November 29, 2016, eighty-six-year-old Aldrin became the oldest human being to reach the South Pole—and he nearly died on the journey. He was traveling in Antarctica, visiting the Amundsen-Scott Science Station, when he came down with a life-threatening lung infection. His National Science Foundation hosts evacuated him to McMurdo Station, then to a hospital in Christchurch, New Zealand, for a week of rest and treatment with antibiotics.

Born on January 20, 1930, in Glen Ridge, New Jersey, as Edwin Eugene Aldrin Jr., Buzz got his nickname from his little sister, who pronounced the word *brother* as "buzzer." His parents soon began calling him Buzz (he took it as his legal name in 1988). Buzz Aldrin was the inspiration for the spaceman character Buzz Lightyear in the animated motion picture *Toy Story*.

After graduating third in his class from the Military Academy at West Point in 1951, Aldrin joined the Air Force, where he flew sixty-six combat missions in the Korean War. He downed two North Korean MiGs and earned the Distinguished Flying Cross. Despite Aldrin's excellent academic and military record, NASA rejected him the first time he applied. But Aldrin was dedicated to his goals. He returned to school and earned a PhD in aeronautics and astronautics at MIT.

In 1963, he reapplied to NASA and was accepted. In the space program, he invented many of the concepts and techniques that have made space exploration possible. He devised procedures for maneuvering, docking, and rendezvousing spacecraft. He originated the practice of simulating low-gravity environments by training underwater. The techniques Aldrin developed enabled him (with astronaut Jim Lovell) to dock Gemini 12 with an unmanned Agena spacecraft and made possible Aldrin's five-and-a-half-hour spacewalk.

The supreme challenge of Aldrin's career came on July 20, 1969, as the Apollo 11 *Eagle* lunar module descended toward the moon. The journey had been problem-plagued ever since the lunar module, carrying astronauts Aldrin and Armstrong, had separated from the command module orbiting the moon. (The third astronaut on the team, Michael Collins, remained in the command module.) The radio link from earth to the lunar module faded in and out. Tracking radar malfunctioned. An alarm sounded, warning the two astronauts that their overloaded landing computer was rebooting.

Then a new crisis arose: as the lunar module was about a mile and a third above the surface, Aldrin and Armstrong saw that their malfunctioning computer was flying them too high, too fast. They were supposed to be approaching a large, smooth landing site. Instead, they had already overflown almost half of the target area. Their present trajectory would drop them in a jagged-rimmed, rubble-strewn crater with boulders the size of railroad boxcars. It was a problem they had never encountered in simulations.

"We heard the call of sixty seconds [of fuel remaining], and a low-level light came on," Aldrin later recalled. "That, I'm sure, caused concern in the control center. They probably normally expected us to land with about two minutes of fuel left. And here we were, still a hundred feet above the surface at sixty seconds. . . . When it got down to thirty seconds, we were about ten feet [above the surface] or less."[1]

Armstrong took over from the computer, using the hand controller to manage *Eagle*'s descent. The computer set off alarms. Aldrin called out speed, altitude, and rate of descent information while Armstrong flew *Eagle* level at four hundred feet over West Crater. Once they had passed the crater, Armstrong resumed the module's descent toward smooth terrain.

The module touched down at 4:18 p.m. EDT, and Armstrong coolly announced, "Houston, Tranquility Base here. The *Eagle* has landed."

The lunar module had about twenty-five to forty seconds' worth of fuel remaining when Armstrong shut down the engine—far less than the two minutes' safety margin mission planners had intended.

The two astronauts remained in the lunar module for a little more than six hours. They decided to skip the five-hour sleep period on the schedule—who could sleep after landing on the moon? They spent those six hours preparing for their moonwalk. During that time, Aldrin radioed a message to the people of the earth: "I'd like to take this opportunity to ask every person listening in, whoever and wherever they may be, to pause for a moment and contemplate the events of the past few hours and to give thanks in his or her own way."[2] Then Aldrin, an elder at the Webster Presbyterian Church of Webster, Texas, took a Holy Communion kit his pastor had given him, and he took Communion on the surface of the moon.

When Armstrong descended the ladder and set foot on the moon, he famously said, "That's one small step for a man, one giant leap for mankind." Aldrin had not prepared any first words for his first footstep on the moon, but when he reached the bottom of the ladder, he turned, gazed at the moonscape, and said the first words that came to mind: "Beautiful, beautiful! Magnificent desolation!"

Buzz Aldrin has lived his life by the twelve West Point virtues, especially the virtue of dedication. He was dedicated to serving his country, dedicated to going to space, dedicated to creating new space travel techniques, dedicated to overcoming any obstacle that got in his way, and dedicated to experiencing everything the universe has to offer, from walking on the moon to walking on the South Pole. His life is a testament to the West Point ideals.

———————— ✦✦✦ ————————

Buzz Aldrin would not have become an astronaut if not for Ed White, West Point class of 1952. White was a year behind Aldrin at the Academy, and they were best friends and teammates on the West Point track team. White enlisted in the air force after graduation and was stationed at Bitburg Air Base in West Germany, where he flew F-86 and F-100 fighter jets in defense of NATO. After Aldrin finished his tour in the Korean War, he was transferred to Bitburg and reunited with Ed White. They routinely flew missions near the Soviet border in planes that bristled with nuclear payloads.

After White's tour in Germany, he earned his master's degree in aeronautical engineering at the University of Michigan. He was dedicated to a career in space travel, and he was committed to taking the practical steps to achieve his goals. White saw that all seven original astronauts selected for NASA's Project Mercury were test pilots. So he went to Edwards Air Force Base in California and enrolled in the Air Force Test Pilot School. When NASA chose the next nine astronauts from among two hundred applicants, White was selected. Once he was in the Gemini program, he urged Aldrin to apply as well.

Edward Higgins White II was born in November 1930 in San Antonio, Texas. He was a Boy Scout and a devout Christian who was active in his local Methodist congregation. A dedicated athlete, White competed for a place on the US Olympic team, hoping to run the 400-meter hurdles in the 1956 Melbourne Games. He was one-tenth of a second short of qualifying.

Aboard Gemini 4 on June 3, 1965, White became the first American astronaut to walk in space. Obsessive about every detail, White checked his camera equipment three times before exiting the capsule, worried he might have left the lens cap on. The EVA (extra-vehicular activity) began during the third orbit while the Gemini capsule was over Hawaii. White remained outside the capsule for twenty-three minutes, using a handheld oxygen-jet "zip gun" to maneuver while attached to the capsule by a tether.

White carried mustard seeds in the pocket of his spacesuit, a symbolic reminder of the words of Jesus in Matthew 17:20: "Truly I tell you, if you have faith as small as a mustard seed, you can say to this mountain, 'Move from here to there,' and it will move. Nothing will be impossible for you."

Once outside the spacecraft, White expressed exhilaration over floating in space. "I feel like a million dollars!" he radioed to crewmate James McDivitt. White's joy while spacewalking made him reluctant to return to the capsule, and Mission Control had to order him back inside. Gemini 4 was over the Gulf of Mexico when White said, "I'm coming back in . . . and it's the saddest moment of my life."[3]

In March 1966, White was named senior pilot (second seat) for the first manned Apollo flight. His crewmates would be Virgil "Gus" Grissom (command pilot), who had previously flown in Mercury and Gemini capsules, and Roger Chaffee (pilot), who had yet to fly in space. The launch of Apollo 1 was scheduled for February 21, 1967.

On January 27, NASA engineers conducted a full rehearsal of the launch sequence with the astronauts strapped into the Apollo 1 capsule at Cape Kennedy's Launchpad 34. One reason for the rehearsal was to practice emergency escape procedures. White's job, as the astronaut in the middle seat, was to ratchet the hatch bolts loose so that all three men could escape in an emergency. During the test, an electrical spark ignited a flash fire, accelerated by the 100 percent oxygen atmosphere. White had no time to open the hatch. His body was found with his arms stretched over his head. He died attempting to save himself and his crewmates. White, Grissom, and Chaffee died of smoke inhalation and asphyxiation.

The tragedy highlighted design flaws in the original Apollo command module, from wiring flaws to the risk of using pressurized oxygen to the poorly designed escape hatch. After NASA's internal review, these defects were fixed, and the Apollo program got back on track.

Ed White was laid to rest at West Point Cemetery with full military honors. In *No Dream Is Too High*, Buzz Aldrin remembered his friendship with fellow West Point cadet Ed White:

> Ed was my good friend and colleague; he was also a major part of my inspiration to become an astronaut. In a couple of minutes, his storied life was over. I never had a chance to thank him for all that he had meant to me, or to tell him goodbye, although two and a half years later, I carried with me to the Moon a medallion in his honor. In some way, I have tried to honor Ed by the path that I have pursued.

Life is a gift, and none of us has any guarantees about tomorrow, so don't miss the opportunity to tell your friends and family members how much they mean to you. Take the time to make that phone call just to say hello, or to write that note of encouragement.[4]

In his wallet, White carried an inspirational poem titled "It's Up to You" by Edgar A. Guest. That poem expressed his intense dedication to his goals and his principles:

> No one is beat till he quits;
>   No one is through till he stops,
> No matter how hard failure hits,
>   No matter how often he drops.
> A fellow's not down till he lies
>   In the dust and refuses to rise.
>
> Fate may slam him and bang him around
>   And batter his frame till he's sore,
> But she never can say that he's downed
>   While he bobs up serenely for more.
> A fellow's not dead till he dies,
>   Nor beat till no longer he tries.[5]

Those words describe the way White lived his life. And they describe the way he died, trying to complete his mission and save his crewmates with his last ounce of strength, with his last breath. He truly exemplified dedication and all the other West Point virtues.

———————— ◆◆◆ ————————

The forgotten astronaut of the Apollo 11 moon shot was another West Point graduate, a classmate of Ed White, Michael Collins, class of 1952. When Neil Armstrong and Buzz Aldrin climbed into the lunar module *Eagle* and separated from the command module *Columbia*, they left Michael Collins behind. He remained in orbit around the moon while Armstrong and Aldrin descended to the Sea of Tranquility.

The moment his two comrades left him, Collins realized just how utterly alone he was, circling the moon, separated from his wife and children, his home world, and the human race by some 240,000 miles of empty space. Soon *Columbia* would swing around behind the moon, and he would lose radio contact with his crewmates and Mission Control. He later confessed that the thought made him a bit panicky.

"Keep talking to me, guys," he radioed to Armstrong and Aldrin. And they talked back and forth by radio until the bulk of the moon blocked their signal.

Collins kept a journal as he orbited. On the far side of the moon, where he couldn't see his distant home world, he wrote, "I am now truly alone and absolutely alone from any known life. I am it."[6]

Armstrong and Aldrin landed safely on the moon. They would spend less than a full day on the lunar surface. Meanwhile, Collins waited, fretted—and sweated. The courage and dedication of the three Apollo 11 astronauts is shown by the fact that all three put the chances of a safe landing and return to earth at about fifty-fifty.

Collins wasn't worried for himself. Instead, he was sick with worry for his two crewmates. "My secret terror for the last six months has been leaving them on the Moon and returning to Earth alone," he wrote in his journal.[7] Collins imagined what would happen if the lunar module lost atmosphere or its engines failed. He would become the lone survivor of the failed Apollo 11 mission—the man who left his buddies on the moon.

Down on the lunar surface, Armstrong and Aldrin collected more than forty-seven pounds of lunar rock and soil and loaded it on the *Eagle*. Aldrin left a bag of memorial items on the surface, including a medallion honoring his late friend Ed White. They took photos, conducted scientific measurements and experiments, inspected the *Eagle* for damage, then pressurized the lunar module and reentered for about seven hours of sleep.

Back on earth, White House speechwriter William Safire had prepared a message for President Richard M. Nixon to deliver if the Apollo 11 voyagers became stranded on the moon. The message read in part, "Fate has ordained that the men who went to the Moon to explore in peace will stay on the Moon to rest in peace. These brave men, Neil Armstrong and Edwin Aldrin, know that there is no hope for their recovery. But they also know that there is hope for mankind in their sacrifice."[8]

After the lunar astronauts reentered the cabin, Aldrin accidentally broke a circuit switch that was part of the main engine starter mechanism. Aldrin worried that he had just stranded them on the moon.

Meanwhile, in lunar orbit, Collins wrote in his journal, "I am within minutes of finding out the truth of the matter. If they fail to rise from the surface, or crash back into it, . . . I will be a marked man for life and I know it."[9]

In the lunar module, Aldrin found he could activate the switch by pushing it into the closed position with a felt-tipped pen. After twenty-one and a half hours on the moon, Armstrong and Aldrin lifted off at 1:54 p.m. EDT in *Eagle*'s ascent stage, bound for an orbital reunion with Collins and *Columbia*.

After the Apollo 11 astronauts returned home, Collins received a letter from famed aviator Charles Lindbergh, the first pilot to fly solo across the Atlantic Ocean in May 1927. Lindbergh, nicknamed "The Lone Eagle," wrote in part:

Dear Colonel Collins,

My congratulations to you on your fascinating, extraordinary, and beautifully executed mission. . . .

What a fantastic experience it must have been—alone looking down on another celestial body, like a god of space! There is a quality of aloneness that those who have not experienced it cannot know—to be alone and then to return to one's fellow men once more. You have experienced an aloneness unknown to man before. I believe you will find that it lets you think and sense with greater clarity. Sometime in the future, I would like to listen to your own conclusions in this respect. . . .

My admiration and my best wishes,

Charles A. Lindbergh[10]

Collins had feared he would be notorious as the lone survivor of Apollo 11. Instead, he ended up being the forgotten Apollo crewmember. Despite his essential role in the success of the mission, his name is rarely mentioned when the first moon landing is recalled. He doesn't mind. He has often said he feels honored to have been a member of the crew of this historic mission. He didn't orbit the moon for fame and glory. He went into space, in the finest tradition of West Point, for duty, honor, country.

Astronaut Frank Borman, West Point class of 1950, was commander of Apollo 8. He and crewmates Jim Lovell and Bill Anders flew the first mission around the moon in December 1968. Borman once told an interviewer, "West Point shaped my life. I have the highest regard for West Point as an institution. Although it has changed a great deal from my day, and I've received a lot of accolades for my work with the space program, nothing makes me more proud than to say I graduated from West Point."[11]

Born in Gary, Indiana, in 1928 and raised in Tucson, Arizona, Borman was a career air force officer, serving as a fighter pilot with the Forty-Fourth Fighter Bomber Squadron in the Philippine Islands, 1951 to 1953, and as a flight instructor in the United States, 1953 to 1956. Borman logged more than six thousand hours of flying time as a military pilot. He returned to West Point in 1957, serving as an assistant professor of thermodynamics and fluid mechanics until 1960. He worked as a test pilot for the USAF Aerospace Research Pilot School for two years, then joined NASA's space program in 1962.

In December 1965, Frank Borman and Jim Lovell flew aboard the two-man Gemini 7 spacecraft, setting a fourteen-day spaceflight endurance record. Gemini 7 rendezvoused in space with Gemini 6A, piloted by Wally Schirra and Thomas P. Stafford. The two crafts came within one foot of each other but did not dock. Borman later recalled, "The Gemini was smaller than the front seat of a Volkswagen bug. So staying in there for fourteen days with another person wasn't easy. But Jim Lovell was great. We got along fine. We never had a bit of trouble."[12]

In late 1966, NASA chose Borman to command the third manned Apollo mission. In January 1967, when the launchpad fire killed Apollo 1 astronauts Grissom, White, and Chaffee, the future of NASA's moon program was in doubt. Borman was appointed to NASA's Accident Review Board.

"After the fire," he recalled, "the head of NASA, Jim Webb, convinced Congress to stay off until NASA had investigated itself. We came up with a report that was very damning because we had frankly overlooked the fact that it was a dangerous test that they were doing.

"Finally, after NASA had made its report, then Congress had a turn at us. And I'll never forget driving over to the Congressional offices where the testimony was to take place. In the car, Jim Webb said to me, 'Now remember, Frank, don't try to protect me, don't try to protect NASA. The American people deserve to know the truth.'

"That was a wonderful example of NASA at its best. And I can't imagine that happening today, as a matter of fact. People would be trying to figure out, 'How do we spin this? How do we make it look good?' But NASA, at that point, was probably as fine a government organization as has ever existed."[13]

Borman's testimony persuaded Congress to allow Apollo to resume its mission. NASA selected Borman to fly in Apollo 8 along with Bill Anders and his Gemini 7 crewmate, Jim Lovell. Apollo 8 went into lunar orbit on Christmas Eve 1968 and made ten orbits around the moon before returning to earth.

"Looking back at the Earth was a profound experience," Borman recalled. "It looked so fragile from 240,000 miles. You have a hard time understanding there could be so much conflict when it looked so fragile."[14]

In preparation for their Christmas Eve broadcast, Borman and Lovell had typed the opening verses of the book of Genesis on their flight plan. In a live broadcast to the world, the three Apollo astronauts took turns reading the first ten verses of the Bible. Anders read first, then Lovell, then Borman, who closed with these words: "And God said, Let the waters under the heaven be gathered together unto one place, and let the dry land appear: and it was so. And God called the dry land Earth; and the gathering together of the waters he called the Seas: and God saw that it was good.' And from the crew of Apollo 8, we close with good night, good luck, a Merry Christmas, and God bless all of you—all of you on the good Earth."[15]

◆━◆━◆

These four astronauts from West Point—Buzz Aldrin, Ed White, Michael Collins, and Frank Borman—exemplify the leadership trait of dedication, the quality of being unwaveringly committed to a purpose that is greater than oneself. Dedication clarifies our goals and the tasks required to achieve them. When you are dedicated to a cause, you never wake up and wonder, *What should I do today?* You *know.* You persevere through opposition, over obstacles, and beyond exhaustion. Your dedication sustains you through every challenge until you achieve your objective.

If you are in business, you dedicate yourself to maintaining the best reputation for excellence and integrity, service to your customers, benefits to your employees, and giving back to your community. If you are in full-time religious service, you dedicate yourself to serving God, spreading his Good News, and ministering to others. If you are in government, you dedicate yourself to defending the Constitution, serving the taxpayers, and making your department run efficiently, with as little waste as possible, for the good of the people, not the bureaucracy. If you are in education, you dedicate yourself to instructing and mentoring your students, instilling values as well as dispensing information, and raising a generation of dedicated leaders.

In 2009, Rachna Choudhry and Marci Harris were discussing the need for a way for Americans to make their opinions known to lawmakers. Choudhry was a political campaign worker with degrees in political science (UCLA) and public policy (Georgetown). Harris was a congressional staffer with expertise in health reform and a law degree from American University. They agreed that the government had become unresponsive to the people.

The following year Choudhry and Harris founded a company called Popvox (after the Latin phrase *vox populi*, "the voice of the people"), with a website at www.popvox.com. It is a place where you can follow your lawmakers, voice your opinions on pending bills, and get personalized updates on legislation at the state and federal level. Choudhry and Harris founded Popvox to be a "transparent advocacy platform" and were gratified with their first success—a grassroots effort to persuade Congress to pay military families during a government shutdown.

In 2012, Popvox CEO Marci Harris told *Fast Company* that the key to the success of Popvox is dedication. She said, "A dedicated team with shared vision is one of the most valuable resources any organization can have—doubly true for a startup. It trumps funding, technology, gold-plated degrees or press. A dedicated team with shared vision can make amazing things happen, and still be standing long after others go home."[16]

What is your great goal in life? What is your equivalent of walking on the moon or traveling to the stars? Whatever you dream of achieving, build the West Point virtue of dedication into your life.

Live each day fully dedicated to the great cause that gives your life meaning and purpose. Be passionate and focused. Live each day dedicated to bettering yourself, becoming stronger, wiser, more knowledgeable, and deeper in character. Always view your life as a work in progress. Keep reading, learning, experiencing, growing, and improving.

Live each day dedicated to being mentored and mentoring others. Recognize the power of influential relationships in your life. When you meet successful people, engage them in conversation. Ask them how they achieved their goals. Ask them the secrets of their success. You will be amazed at how eager people are to share their wisdom and help others succeed.

Live each day dedicated to the future, not the past. Don't settle for conformity. Don't settle for the status quo. Be an agent of positive change in the lives of others, and the world around you. Push the boundaries of imagination. Don't accept what is; dream of what might be—then find ways to make it happen.

Live each day dedicated to lifting others up. Ed White wanted to uplift his friend Buzz Aldrin, so he persistently urged Buzz to become an astronaut. Because of White, who gave his life reaching for the moon, Aldrin walked on the moon and left a medallion in the moondust to honor White. Michael Collins wanted to uplift his friends Neil Armstrong and Buzz Aldrin, and he was content to be the forgotten man in the orbiting command module while they got the glory of leaving footprints on the moon. Collins's greatest terror was that he would have to go home alone. And none of these astronauts would have gone to the moon if not for Frank Borman's candid testimony to Congress about the Apollo 1 tragedy—testimony that enabled NASA to continue reaching for the sky.

Remember the four West Point astronauts. As you ascend in your career, in your faith, in your education, dedicate yourself to uplifting others. Remember the West Point virtues, especially the virtue of dedication. Aim high, reach for the stars, and fulfill the purpose for which God made you.

Leave footprints in the universe that will stand the test of time.

4

DETERMINATION

NEVER GIVE UP

Every day Maggie Dixon went to work she drew inspiration from the words of General Douglas MacArthur inscribed over the entrance to the West Point gymnasium: "Upon the fields of friendly strife are sown the seeds that upon other fields, on other days, will bear the fruits of victory."

Dixon was twenty-eight years old when she was hired as the head women's basketball coach at the United States Military Academy at West Point. She had spent five years as an assistant coach and recruiter under Doug Bruno at DePaul University in Chicago but had never been a head coach before. The thought of coaching at West Point was intimidating. Since Dixon had never been in the military, she wasn't sure she would fit in.

She called her brother, Jamie Dixon, head coach of the men's basketball team at the University of Pittsburgh, and asked his advice. He gave her the same advice he had given her five years earlier, when she had applied at DePaul: "Just be yourself."

Maggie Dixon took her brother's advice and met the challenge head-on, approaching the job at West Point with an air of absolute confidence. Her bold attitude, Jamie later said, "tells you everything you want to know about Maggie Dixon."[1]

Jamie and Maggie were always close as brother and sister. She looked up to him, and he nurtured her interest in basketball. When Maggie was twelve, Jamie registered her for a summer basketball camp and drove her there, thinking she would meet other girls who shared her love of the sport. It turned out there were 150 boys at the camp—and Maggie was the only girl. Jamie asked her if she wanted to back out. But Maggie was determined to improve her skills—and through her confident and charming personality, she became the camp hero.

By the time she was in college, Maggie Dixon was nearly six feet in height. She played starting forward at the University of San Diego. After college, she tried out to play in the WNBA but didn't make the cut. Undaunted, she called her brother and said, "I want to do what you do. I'm going to drive to Chicago and get a job in coaching."

So she and a friend got in her car and drove two thousand miles from California to Chicago. There was no job listing, and she didn't phone ahead to make an appointment. She had mailed her résumé weeks earlier but had heard nothing back. She was going to Chicago to ask for a job, and she was determined not to take no for an answer.

Dixon and her friend arrived at the DePaul University campus on a Friday in May 2000. They went to Alumni Hall, the 5,308-seat arena for DePaul women's sports (it was torn down and replaced in 2001). Dixon found a custodian and said, "I'd like to speak with Coach Bruno, please."

The custodian found Doug Bruno in the showers and told him there was a tall young lady who wanted to talk to him in the arena. Bruno had plans for the evening—but what if the tall young lady was his next star player? Coach Bruno dressed and went out to meet her. She put out her hand and said, "I'm Maggie Dixon. Will you hire me as your assistant?"

"I'm sorry. We don't have any openings."

"I drove all the way from San Diego. Could I have an interview?"

"Okay. How's nine o'clock tomorrow morning? I can give you ten minutes."[2]

Dixon arrived promptly at nine. She and Coach Bruno talked—not for ten minutes but for three hours. At the end of that conversation, Dixon was Coach Bruno's new assistant. The job would entail hard work, long hours, and starvation wages. She eagerly accepted.

To make ends meet, Dixon took a second job waiting tables at a steak house. She did much of her shopping at a thrift store. The following year Dixon was promoted to a full-time assistant coach and no longer had to wait tables. The year after that she was also the team's recruiting coordinator.

When Dixon heard about the head coaching job at West Point, she called Jamie and asked if he thought she should apply. "Go for it," he said. She did—and she got the job. She was hired just eleven days before the start of the 2005–6 season, so she had to hit the ground running.

She began by trying to teach her cadets the inverted flex offense. The result was that her Army Black Knights struggled to a 5–7 record in their first dozen games. She decided she had overcomplicated the game, so she switched to a simpler offense. As a result, practices became more enjoyable for the players, and games became more winnable.

Dixon became close with her players, cooking pancake breakfasts and dinners for them, taking them bowling, and sharing their joys and frustrations. During the six months she coached them, she had a big impact on their game and an even bigger impact on their lives. Her players felt that she was not only their coach but also their mentor and friend.

In everything she attempted, Dixon's approach was to go after what she wanted, never give up, and never take no for an answer. She was determination personified. During those first dozen games, Dixon saw how hard it was for players to keep their confidence and enthusiasm high when the stands were empty. The Black Knights needed a cheering section at home games—that all-important "sixth man" to give the team an emotional lift. She went to the mess hall one day, stood up in front of all the cadets, both men and women, clanged a spoon against a glass to get everyone's attention, then said, "Beat Navy! I want to see you cadets—and I mean the male cadets—coming to our women's games. And I want you to raise the rafters and lift up our team!"[3]

It was a short speech, but it was effective. Male cadets showed up at the games, and they cheered and stomped and raised the rafters. The women of West Point began playing at a whole new level—and they began to win. After a poor 5–7 start, the Black Knights finished with a record of 20–11. Maggie Dixon was named Patriot League coach of the year.

The Black Knights had their biggest game against Holy Cross in the Patriot League tournament final at West Point's Christl Arena. In the closing minutes of a tight game, Dixon sent in a sophomore forward who had gotten very little playing time all season. "I believe in you so much," Dixon told Stefanie Stone. "Take a deep breath and have fun."

Stone went into the game, and Holy Cross fouled her with eight seconds left to play. The game was tied 68–68 as Stone went to the free throw line. She missed her first shot. Stone looked at her coach, and Dixon nodded confidently. Stone put up the second shot—and it was good.

Army won, 69 to 68, and clinched the Patriot League Conference. Hundreds of male cadets with painted faces ran out onto the court, lifted Dixon on their shoulders, and carried her around the arena in triumph. The Black Knights had won their first title ever. Next stop, the NCAA tournament.

In March 2006, Jamie Dixon and Maggie Dixon both headed to Madison Square Garden for the tournament—the first brother and sister to take their teams to the Big Dance. The Black Knights suffered a painful loss to Tennessee in the first round of that tournament, but just getting there was an amazing achievement. It was the first time any army basketball team, men's or women's, had ever played in the NCAA tournament. After the game, Maggie Dixon went home to prepare for the next season.

Tragically, however, there would be no next season for Dixon.

On April 5, 2006, she was having tea in the home of a friend when she fell unconscious. An ambulance took her to Westchester Medical Center in Valhalla, New York. Her brother, sister, and parents flew in to be at her side, but Dixon never regained consciousness. She died the following night. An autopsy revealed that she had a previously undiagnosed enlarged heart.

She was buried on a rainy Good Friday with a military ceremony at West Point Cemetery. The superintendent of West Point, Lieutenant General William J. Lennox Jr., memorialized Dixon, saying, "Her presence is what really struck us. That's the impact a leader can have and, in a house of leaders, she stood out."[4]

In October 2009, I had the privilege of speaking at West Point and walking the grounds where Generals Ulysses S. Grant, "Black Jack" Pershing, Douglas MacArthur, and Dwight D. Eisenhower walked. My host was Ralph Pim, the head of the Academy's physical education department. He took me to West Point Cemetery, and I visited Maggie Dixon's grave. Her headstone reads:

MAGGIE DIXON
May 9, 1977–April 5, 2006
Beloved Daughter, Sister, and Aunt
Women's Basketball Head Coach, 2005–2006
So Good, So Wise, So Young

Dixon's grave is visited by cadets, coaches, journalists, and others who knew her only by reputation. People leave mementos to honor her—basketballs, coins, stones, pins, ribbons, and more. Why do people feel compelled to leave something of themselves at her grave? I think doing so is more than just a tribute to a famous lady. It is an attempt by admirers to reach out and connect with leadership greatness. It is an attempt to touch and absorb some of her determined spirit, the spirit of a woman who refused to take no for an answer.

◆━◆●◆━◆

H. Norman Schwarzkopf, West Point class of 1956, was Commander in Chief, United States Central Command, from 1988 to 1991. He oversaw the largest deployment of American forces since the Vietnam War, including portions of the US Army, Navy, Air Force, and Marine Corps, and integrated those forces with units from dozens of nations around the world. He planned and directed the ground assault known as Operation Desert Storm, a military operation that lasted one hundred hours and resulted in the surrender of the Iraqi Army. That operation earned him the nickname "Stormin' Norman." He passed away in 2012.

Years ago, General Schwarzkopf spoke at a spring gala fundraiser sponsored by the Orlando Magic Youth Foundation. I was the general's host for the evening and was honored to spend time talking with him. He was outgoing, friendly, and engaging.

"General," I said, "do you ever think that a madman in Iraq, and his decision to invade Kuwait, helped make you a household name?"

"I think about it all the time," he said. "If it hadn't been for Saddam Hussein, no one would ever have heard of me."

General Schwarzkopf was a confident, compelling public speaker. I asked him, "What's the most important step you've taken to improve yourself as a speaker?"

"I realized I was being held back by note cards," he said. "I determined to become a more natural speaker. I threw away my

74

note cards, came out from behind the lectern, and started talking to audiences the way you and I are talking right now."

It occurred to me that he became a more natural, extemporaneous speaker the same way he did everything else in his life: through decisiveness and determination. Whether he was speaking from the heart to an audience in Orlando, Florida, or commanding one of the biggest military operations in history, or saving a company of soldiers in the jungles of Vietnam, determination was the key to his success.

On May 28, 1970, Lieutenant Colonel Schwarzkopf was almost at the end of his second tour of duty in Vietnam. Word came to him that a unit under his command, Bravo Company, had entered a minefield and set off a mine. Two soldiers were down. Schwarzkopf immediately boarded a helicopter and flew to the minefield.

He arrived to find Bravo Company paralyzed with fear, unable to move forward or backward. The helicopter took the two wounded soldiers away, leaving Schwarzkopf and his artillery officer, Tom Bratton, behind. Schwarzkopf and Bratton conferred with the company commander, trying to figure out how to rescue the men of Bravo Company. As they talked, a mine exploded, blowing one soldier into the air. The man's leg snapped when he hit the ground, and he thrashed about in pain.

Other soldiers yelled in panic. Schwarzkopf knew that panic was contagious. He also feared that the wounded man might open an artery and bleed out. Someone had to get to him and calm him down. Schwarzkopf recalled:

> I was the senior ranking man there and it was my responsibility. Besides that, I wanted the company commander, who was standing next to me, to . . . get his leadership working, talk to them and get the company calmed down. So I went over to help this kid. . . . I got over to the kid. I was a pretty big guy then, as I am now, and I laid down on top of him. I literally pinned him and was talking to him, saying, "Come on, you've got to calm down now. You're

going to cut an artery. You're going to kill yourself. You're scaring the hell out of all the rest of the troops." . . . And I got the kid calmed down.[5]

Schwarzkopf turned to his artillery officer, Tom Bratton, and said, "Cut a limb off that bush and throw it to me so I can splint this guy's leg." Bratton turned to do so—and set off a mine. When the smoke cleared, Bratton lay on the ground, an arm and a leg traumatically amputated. He bled profusely from his head, but he was alive. The mine had exploded in the helicopter landing zone, which had been thought safe.

Schwarzkopf's chest bled. He had been hit by shrapnel. The men in the minefield continued screaming for help.

"Stand where you are!" Schwarzkopf shouted. "We're going to get you out!" He removed his belt and lashed the wounded man's legs together to immobilize the broken bone.

Then he crept over to Bratton. Schwarzkopf and the company commander bandaged and put a tourniquet on Bratton's wounds. A medevac helicopter came to take the wounded men away.

Schwarzkopf called for engineers to come and mark the mines to make a safe path. He also told headquarters to send as many cans of shaving cream as they had. "And don't argue with me," he added. "Just get that shaving cream here now!"

The engineers arrived with the shaving cream, and Schwarzkopf directed them to clear a safe path with metal detectors, using a dollop of white shaving cream to mark the locations of the mines. The shaving cream was too light to trigger the mine but remained visible for hours.

Years later, Schwarzkopf recalled, "When the last kid was off the hill, I had them fly me to the hospital. After they dug seven or eight pieces of shrapnel out of my left pectoral muscle and bandaged me up, I bullied the doctor into letting me go."[6]

Lieutenant Colonel Schwarzkopf went to that minefield with an iron determination to bring every man back alive—and he did.

Schwarzkopf's improvised shaving cream idea later became the accepted means of marking land mines in battlefields in Iraq and Afghanistan.

Determination is a West Point virtue every leader needs, especially when facing crises, obstacles, and opposition. Determination means making up your mind that you will achieve your goal. You will not give up. You will not accept defeat. You will not take no for an answer.

If you do not make an ironclad decision to attack your objective with absolute determination, you may find yourself surrendering to indecision, uncertainty, hesitation, or paralysis. The determined mind expects roadblocks and obstacles, but it is prepared to find a way over, around, or straight through them. The virtue of determination helps you focus your energy on the problem with laser-like intensity.

Whether you are a business leader trying to navigate a turbulent economy, a coach trying to find a way to win a basketball game, or a military leader trying to save the lives of your soldiers, you need iron-willed determination to achieve your goals. There must not be an ounce of "quit" in you. You must find a way to keep going.

Determination made Norman Schwarzkopf a legendary leader. Determination made Maggie Dixon a coaching legend in a single season. The West Point virtue of determination will serve you well in your leadership arena and enable you to build an enduring legacy.

5

DIGNITY

EVERY INCH A SOLDIER

"Black Jack" Pershing, West Point class of 1886, might never have had such a legendary military career if he had not known how to parse the sentence "I love to run."

Born on a farm in Missouri on September 13, 1860, young John J. Pershing wasn't planning a career in the military while attending State Normal School in Kirksville, Missouri. He was studying to be a teacher, but he really wanted to become a lawyer. He believed that the education he received at Normal in rural Missouri was substandard, but he couldn't afford the kind of education that would prepare him for a career in law.

One day while reading the weekly newspaper, he saw an announcement for an examination to be held in Trenton,

Missouri, "for the purpose of selecting one Cadet for the Military Academy at West Point." The Academy, he knew, was one of the highest-ranked academic institutions in the country, and West Point cadets were trained not only as soldiers but also as gentlemen, well qualified for any civilian profession as well as a military profession. Most important of all, an education at West Point was free.

Pershing's sister Elizabeth—he called her Bessie—helped him cram for the examination, asking him question after question on a wide variety of subjects. Night after night for two weeks, Bessie quizzed John until he felt his mind was about to burst.

On the day of the examination, Pershing arrived at the examination room—and his heart sank to see dozens of other young men who had come to compete for a nomination to West Point. The examiners handed out written questions to the applicants. Pershing found the exam difficult, yet he was pleased to find that the cramming sessions with Bessie had paid off. Many of the questions on the exam covered subjects he had thoroughly studied beforehand. Eventually, the examiners announced that time was up, and Pershing turned in his paper along with the rest of the applicants. Sometime later, the examiners returned and announced that two applicants had tied for first place, C. W. Chapman and John Pershing. The tie would be broken by an oral exam.

Chapman and Pershing were questioned by a panel of examiners. Both men demonstrated equal mastery of geography. Next subject: English grammar. The two men were asked to parse the sentence "I love to run." Both Chapman and Pershing identified "I" as the subject. Both selected "love" as the verb. Chapman identified "to run" as an adverb qualifying the verb "love." Pershing identified "to run" as the object of the verb. The examiners offered Pershing a congratulatory handshake. He had won the nomination to West Point.

West Point is unlike any other institution of higher learning. No other school instills such a deep and almost spiritual sense of belonging, tradition, and loyalty as the Military Academy at West Point. I have walked among its stone halls and buildings, its parade grounds, its library and chapel, and its cemetery. Buildings and halls, walkways and greens are all named for West Point alumni, heroes all, many of whom fell in battle. The place is drenched in history and tradition, and all that history becomes the heritage of every cadet who passes through its gates. Every cadet is a brother or sister in arms not only to their classmates but also to the generations of cadets who came before and those who will come after. That heritage was instilled into the heart and soul of John J. Pershing from the moment he arrived in the fall of 1882.

At West Point, Pershing showed a strong aptitude for leadership and quickly rose to the highest cadet rank, first captain. When the funeral train of President Ulysses S. Grant passed by West Point in August 1885, First Captain Pershing commanded the West Point honor guard. One of the qualities that distinguished Cadet Pershing from his peers was the aura of dignity he projected at all times.

Pershing's biographer, Frank Everson Vandiver, wrote that Cadet Pershing's air of dignified maturity "set him out from his comrades. He was more a man than the rest."[1] One of Pershing's classmates, Robert Lee Bullard, observed that Pershing was "plainly of the estate of man while most of those about him were still boys." The other cadets, Vandiver wrote, "saw things they liked in classmate Pershing, things to admire. Most of them knew he had a dignity and dependability beyond their grasp. Admiration was the reaction he most often inspired."[2]

Midway through Pershing's first year at West Point, his fellow first-year classmates honored him by electing him class president. He did not seek the office or expect to be honored in this way, and no other candidates ran against him. He was elected by unanimous acclamation, and he held the position for life. Whenever there was a reunion of the West Point class of 1886, Pershing's classmates looked up to him as their leader.

Before the start of Pershing's final year at West Point, his superior officers gave him the distinct honor of making him senior captain of the Corps of Cadets—the highest honor a West Pointer can earn. They recognized that Pershing was a leader and a role model for all other cadets to emulate. Pershing exemplified the virtues of West Point, particularly the virtue of dignity.

As senior captain, Pershing was in charge of all cadet ceremonies and official occasions, and he hosted many visiting VIPs. One frequent guest lecturer at West Point was novelist Mark Twain. Pershing enjoyed meeting Twain, a fellow Missouri native. After a lecture to the cadets, Twain relaxed with Pershing and several classmates in Pershing's room at the barracks. Twain spent more than an hour telling stories of the fascinating people he had met in his travels. It was an afternoon Pershing never forgot.

The superintendent of the Academy at that time was a distinguished Civil War officer, Colonel Wesley Merritt of the cavalry. Pershing later recalled that Colonel Merritt's friends included "Grant, Sherman, Sheridan, and other great soldiers of the Civil War, several of whom came to visit West Point during my cadet days. I remember especially the stately figure of General Sherman as he took his daily walk about the post and how we used to consider it an especial honor to salute him."[3]

Ranked thirtieth in a class of seventy-seven cadets, Pershing graduated from West Point on June 11, 1886. He was commissioned as a second lieutenant in the army and posted to the Sixth Cavalry at Fort Bayard in the New Mexico Territory. He later served at posts in Arizona, California, and North Dakota.

From 1891 to 1895, Pershing taught military science and tactics at the University of Nebraska at Lincoln. While there, he attended the College of Law, completing his law degree in 1893. Two years later, he was promoted to first lieutenant and placed in command of the Tenth Cavalry Regiment, a "Buffalo Soldier" regiment composed entirely of African American troops.

Pershing's Nebraska students admired him, even emulated him. They were impressed, above all, by his soldierly dignity. As Pershing's biographer observed, "He put his stamp on all of his men. They copied his walk, his flat midwestern drawl, his mannerisms. They talked about him almost constantly, vied to praise and assess him: 'We loved him devotedly'; 'Every inch of him was a soldier'; 'I have never seen a man with such poise, dignity, and personality.'"[4]

In 1897, the army appointed Pershing to the West Point staff as an instructor. Though he had many admirers, he also earned the displeasure of quite a few West Point cadets due to the strict discipline he imposed. It was during this time that cadets gave him the nickname "Black Jack." It was intended as an insult and was spoken only behind his back. When Pershing learned of the nickname, he encouraged its use. By the time of World War I, even the newspapers had begun calling him "Black Jack" Pershing.

The Spanish-American War began in April 1898. Lieutenant Pershing fought in Cuba and was cited for gallantry in the battles of Kettle Hill and San Juan Hill. In fact, Pershing's calm, dignified, commanding leadership on San Juan Hill earned him a captaincy and the praise of General Theodore A. Baldwin, who later said, "I have been in many fights in the Civil War, but Captain Pershing is the coolest man under fire I ever saw in my life."[5]

Captain Charles S. Ayres commanded Troop E of the Tenth Cavalry during the battle of San Juan Hill. He recalled, "As we approached San Juan Creek, Troop E was in the lead of the Tenth Cavalry. When we got to the Creek, the order was brought by the gallant Pershing, who was as cool as a bowl of cracked ice, for the troops to take cover along the creek and await further orders. Into the Creek we went after the courteous Pershing, who was showing us where to go."[6]

Meanwhile, half a world away, the United States Navy's Asiatic Squadron steamed out of Hong Kong under the command of Commodore George Dewey, bound for the Philippine Islands. On May 1, 1898, Dewey's forces engaged—and sank—Spain's Pacific Squadron in the Battle of Manila Bay. Dewey then blockaded the port of Manila. By August, American forces had captured Manila and established a military government with Major General Wesley Merritt as the first American military governor. The United States wrested possession of the Philippines from Spain, which had colonized the Philippines three centuries earlier, and the Spanish-American War came to an end.

A group of Filipino revolutionaries, who had been at war for several years with Spain over Spanish rule of the islands, proclaimed themselves the revolutionary government of the Philippines. They adopted a constitution and appointed a president—thirty-year-old Emilio Aguinaldo—to head the First Philippine Republic. Their goal was to free the Philippines from American rule. The war between the US and the Filipino nationalists became known as the Philippine-American War, which was fought until the Filipinos surrendered in 1902.

John J. Pershing, with the rank of major in the United States Volunteers, was posted to Manila in August 1899. He was cited for gallantry in the battle for the Filipinos' stronghold at Macajambo. The American cavalry struggled to bring field guns by mule along a narrow trail through the dense jungle and steep terrain of a river valley. When the Americans reached the Macajambo fortress, they faced stiff resistance. The guns of the fortress had a commanding view of the valley approaches, and the well-armed Filipinos kept the Americans pinned down, unable to attempt an assault.

Pershing conferred with the commander of the cavalry unit, Brigadier General William Birkhimer, and pointed out that the fortress sat at the mouth of a gorge and was flanked on two sides by steep cliffs. Pershing offered to take fifteen men to the top of one cliff, while Captain Jim Mays took a second group of fifteen men to the top of the other cliff. Birkhimer approved the plan. Hours later, Pershing and Mays had their sharpshooters spread out atop the two cliffs, and they proceeded to send a hail of lead into the fort from above. By sunset, the guns of the fortress had fallen silent. The next day the American field guns blasted away at the walls of the fort, and the remaining defenders fled into the jungle. The army cited Pershing for gallantry in leading the attack that led to victory at Macajambo.

Pershing left the Philippines and served in several posts, including military attaché in Tokyo and military observer in the Balkans. In 1905, he married Helen Frances Warren, daughter of Senator Francis E. Warren of Wyoming. That same year President Theodore Roosevelt nominated Pershing for the rank of brigadier general, moving him three steps higher in rank in a single move. Congress approved the nomination, and Pershing returned to the Philippines in 1909.

After the Americans had quelled resistance in the Catholic northern Philippines, they faced a different situation in the southern islands of Mindanao and the Sulu Archipelago, which had substantial Muslim populations. The Muslim Filipinos were called Moros (Spanish for Moors). When the US attempted to assert its authority over the southern islands, the Moro Rebellion broke out, a guerrilla war not unlike wars America has fought in Vietnam and Afghanistan.

In 1909, Pershing was assigned as military governor of the Moro Province, the largely Muslim southern region of the Philippines. His goal was to bring stability, commerce, prosperity, and peace to the southern islands. To accomplish this goal, he had to end the reign of Moro violence and terror. "Life and property were safe nowhere in the interior of the Province," Pershing recalled in his autobiography. "Especially in Jolo, owners of carabao, cattle, and horses had often to stand guard over them day and night. . . . The long list of murders and assassinations committed by Moros and pagans since the establishment of provincial government brought discredit upon the Province and made it unsafe, except in municipalities where the Filipino population predominated."[7]

He recalled one incident in which an American cavalry officer, Lieutenant W. H. Rodney, was walking near his barracks with his five-year-old daughter when a Moro terrorist, who had come to the barracks to kill Americans, approached the lieutenant from behind and hacked him to death in front of his terrified little girl. The commanding officer of the unit called out the guard, who shot the killer before he could hurt anyone else.

Because of this and other acts of senseless violence, Pershing instituted a two-year campaign against the Moro outlaws. In that time, Pershing's troops—a combined force of American and Filipino soldiers—shut down ten Moro crime rings, killed one hundred twenty-six outlaws, and arrested nearly a hundred more.

In recent years, an internet meme has spread claiming that Black Jack Pershing brought peace to the Philippines by executing captured Muslim terrorists with bullets dipped in the blood of pigs (a forbidden animal among Muslims). The terrorists were supposedly so frightened of being sent to hell by the pork-tainted bullets that they put down their weapons and learned to behave. Though the story is false and has been widely debunked, it continues to circulate on the internet.

The myth of the bullets dipped in pig blood may be a greatly distorted version of an account in Pershing's autobiography. He said that fanatical Moro assassins called *juramentados* sometimes attacked Americans knowing they would be shot and killed (not unlike suicide bombers today). Pershing described the solution the army implemented to curb the violence:

These *juramentado* attacks were materially reduced in number by a practice the army had already adopted, one that Muhammadans held in abhorrence. The bodies were publicly buried in the same grave with a dead pig. It was not pleasant to take such measures, but the prospect of going to hell instead of heaven sometimes deterred the would-be assassins.[8]

Pershing himself never ordered such burials, but he was aware of them. He found them regrettable but felt they helped reduce the number of innocent deaths. In fact, Daniel Immerwahr, assistant professor of history at Northwestern University, wrote:

Pershing proved remarkably sympathetic toward Filipino Muslims, called "Moros," as a whole. He made diplomatic visits to them, making a point of going unarmed. He ate their food, learned their customs, and counted some as "strong personal friends." He studied their language to the point where, he boasted, he could take low-level meetings without an interpreter. In return, Pershing was elected a *datu*, a position of respect and leadership in Moro society. He was the only US official to be so honored.[9]

In his autobiography, Pershing described his respect for the dignity of the Moro people and their customs. He recalled a meeting at the fortified palace of a Moro patriarch named Sajiduciaman. There Pershing and his staff met a large number of Moros, led by sultans and *dattos*. "After showing me about the interior with great dignity," Pershing wrote, "the patriarch brought me back to the gathering of Moros and American troops outside."

The Americans stood at attention, sounded bugles, raised the American flag, and fired an artillery salute as a show of respect and power. Pershing and the patriarch squatted on their heels with the crowd of Moros and Americans in a circle around them. A Moro servant brought out a Koran and solemnly placed it on a mat in front of an "aged Muhammadan priest in gorgeous trousers of many colors and a robe of yellow silk," attended by a slave with a red parasol.

The patriarch and Pershing each made ceremonial speeches, and the Moro chiefs placed their hands on the Koran and vowed "friendship and allegiance to the United States." Pershing respected the Moro ceremony. He concluded, "This gathering of brilliantly arrayed warriors and people of the East with khaki-uniformed troops from the West, in a setting of nature's magnificence, a glorious tropical sky overhead, the silvery lake shimmering below, the primeval forests and towering mountains in the background, was history made visible in most picturesque fashion."[10]

The Library of Congress contains a transcript of a meeting between Pershing, governor of the Moro Province, and local Muslim leaders. Pershing referred to the Muslims as "my old friends" and told them, "The Moros of Lake Lanao are undoubtedly aware of the fact that from the very first days of American occupation here there has been no interference with their religion. . . . I wish to state that this is not the country of the Americans, but is the country of you Moros, and we are not going to bring here Americans to push you out."

As Daniel Immerwahr concluded, "It's an admirable sentiment, brimming with tolerance for a foreign culture."[11] It is also the statement of a man who not only maintained his own dignity, in accordance with West Point virtues, but also demonstrated respect for the dignity of other people, other religions, and other cultures.

<hr />

At the end of 1913, General Pershing took command of the Eighth Brigade at the Presidio in San Francisco. The brigade deployed to Fort Bliss, Texas, in April 1914. General Pershing spent more than a year away from his family and was looking forward to bringing his wife and four children to be with him at Fort Bliss. Then on August 27, 1915, he received a telegram informing him of a tragedy. A lacquered floor at the Presidio had caught fire, trapping his family. His wife, Helen, and his three daughters, ages three, seven, and eight, had died of smoke inhalation. Only his six-year-old son had escaped. After the funerals in Cheyenne, Wyoming, General Pershing returned to Fort Bliss with his son and his sister May. He dealt with his grief by resuming his duties.

In March 1916, General Pershing commanded the Mexican Punitive Expedition, a force of ten thousand troops that pursued Pancho Villa and his band of revolutionaries, but failed to capture him. One of Pershing's most trusted officers on that expedition was a young Lieutenant George S. Patton. The lieutenant led a force of three Dodge touring cars and fifteen soldiers on a raid near Rubio, Chihuahua. Three leaders in the Pancho Villa band were shot and killed by the Americans as they shot from the moving vehicles. It was the first motorized attack in the history of American warfare.

Patton returned to General Pershing's headquarters with three dead bandits strapped to the hoods of the three touring cars. That day General Pershing nicknamed Lieutenant Patton "Bandito."

◆━◆━◆━◆

The United States under President Woodrow Wilson entered World War I in May 1917. After a brief interview with General Pershing at the White House, President Wilson decided to place Pershing in command of the army. On October 6, the army promoted Pershing from major general to four-star general, bypassing the three-star lieutenant general rank. Pershing's job was to bring America's armed forces to a state of readiness and direct those forces in the war in Europe. Pershing began with twenty-seven thousand green, untested troops, some voluntary, some draftees, some from the army, some from the National Guard. By the end of the war, Pershing had miraculously transformed that small band of soldiers into a well-trained, highly disciplined force of two million men.

Having previously commanded African American "Buffalo Soldiers" of the Tenth Cavalry Regiment, Pershing had great respect for the African American soldiers in his army. He would have liked to integrate the army, but he knew that many white soldiers in the army harbored racial bias and were not ready to accept integration. President Wilson also held regressive views on race, as did the southern Democrats who supported him. So General Pershing maintained the status quo of "separate but equal" African American companies and battalions in the army.

General Pershing's forces arrived in France in June 1917. Pershing demonstrated the American arrival by sending troops marching through Paris. They were greeted with cheering crowds. Pershing and his aide, Colonel Charles Stanton, paused by the tomb of the Marquis de Lafayette, the French military strategist who aided George Washington in the American Revolutionary War. Colonel Stanton, awed by the great symbolism of that moment as Americans came to the aid of France, softly said, "Lafayette, we are here." For decades afterward, those words would be misattributed to Pershing himself.

The Americans fought fiercely throughout the war, taking heavy losses but lifting the morale of the war-weary British and French forces, who had been fighting since 1914. In all, more than seventy million military personnel were mobilized in this "war to end all wars." More than nine million combatants and seven million civilians were killed in the war.

On November 11, 1918, Allied and German delegates met in a railroad carriage at Compiègne in northern France. They signed an armistice agreement providing a cease-fire that would take effect at "the eleventh hour of the eleventh day of the eleventh month." The war was over, and General John J. "Black Jack" Pershing came home to a hero's welcome.

In 1919, the United States Congress authorized President Wilson to promote Pershing to the rank of general of the Armies of the United States—the highest military rank possible, created especially for General Pershing.

In 1920, the Republican Party sought to draft General Pershing as its candidate for president to run against Wilson, but Pershing declined the honor. He chose, instead, to serve as chief of staff for the army, a position he held for three years. During that time, he foresaw the need for a system of roadways traversing the length and breadth of the United States, for both military and civilian traffic. He drew up what came to be called the Pershing Map, which bears a striking resemblance to the Interstate Highway System championed by President Dwight D. Eisenhower and authorized by the Federal Aid Highway Act of 1956.

General Pershing retired from active military service on September 13, 1924, his sixty-fourth birthday. He faded into private life, gone but not forgotten. He briefly experienced renewed celebrity status when he published his memoirs, *My Experiences in the World War*, which won the Pulitzer Prize for history in 1932. Then he retreated into quiet obscurity once more.

In October 1942, General George S. Patton Jr. was preparing to mobilize twenty-four thousand men for a landing near Casablanca, Morocco. Before leaving America to join his troops, Patton went to Walter Reed Army Hospital to visit his mentor, "Black Jack" Pershing. The eighty-two-year-old General Pershing told his protégé, "I am happy they are sending you to the front at once. I like generals who are so bold that they are dangerous."

Patton thanked Pershing for all he had learned while serving under Pershing in Mexico. Then Patton knelt at Pershing's bedside, kissed the old man's hand, and asked for his blessing.

Pershing gripped Patton's hand and said, "God bless and keep you and give you victory."[12]

Patton stood, snapped off a salute, and walked out of the general's hospital room—off to help win the next great war.

John J. "Black Jack" Pershing, General of the Armies of the United States, died on July 15, 1948, at Walter Reed Army Hospital.

He was laid to rest at Arlington National Cemetery among the soldiers he had led in World War I. He was every inch a soldier, and his tombstone is inscribed with the same simple dignity that marked his life:

JOHN J. PERSHING
Missouri
General of the Armies of the United States
September 13, 1860
July 15, 1948

Dignity was once a highly prized virtue in our culture. People valued their own dignity and respected the dignity of others. Today, our entertainment, our literature, our conversations at work and on the street, and our political discourse have all been coarsened by disrespect for one another and even for ourselves. America was once led by statesmen such as Washington and Lincoln, who elevated and dignified the office they held. Today, we are forced to choose among candidates who engage in name-calling, school yard taunts, and indecent behavior.

The word *dignity* comes from the Latin word *dignitas*, meaning "worthiness." When we speak and act in a dignified way, we demonstrate our own worthiness, our own human worth. When we respect and defend the dignity of other people, we value their human worth. Marcus Aurelius, a Stoic philosopher and the last of the five good emperors of Rome, observed in *Meditations*, book IV, "There is a proper dignity and proportion to be observed in the performance of every act of life."[13] Dignity is a priceless virtue—a virtue that is in danger of extinction in our society.

We maintain our dignity by good conduct and good manners, by remaining calm and poised under pressure, by being thoughtful instead of emotional, by maintaining self-control (especially when others are losing control), by accepting setbacks and disappointments with grace, by demonstrating excellence in everything we do and say, and by respecting others.

All human beings have a right to have their dignity respected and protected. One of the worst things one human being can do to another is to humiliate that person, to rob that person of their God-given dignity. The foundation of most moral precepts is the notion that all human beings have an inherent right to be treated with dignity.

Carrie Kerpen, cofounder and CEO of Likeable Media, told the story of a woman executive who visited a branch office to find out why the office wasn't meeting performance expectations. After investigating, she decided that the people in the branch office needed to be confronted and corrected. "I just went in and I was the boss," she said later. She didn't respect the dignity of the people in that office, and many were hurt and humiliated by her actions.

One employee took the executive aside and privately told her that he had previously had an excellent relationship with the company. He felt as if he were "married" to the company. By coming in and humiliating him, robbing him of his dignity, this executive had broken up his "marriage" to the company. The relationship would never be the same. The trust was broken.

Kerpen said the executive learned a big lesson from that incident. Now, whenever she has to correct or confront an employee, her attitude is always, "I am here to safeguard your dignity in this conversation." The executive told Kerpen, "You want people to feel that you came, you inspired, you instructed, you fixed things, but you did it with dignity—and treated others with the respect that everyone deserves."[14]

Writing for *Fast Company*, author and business consultant Bud Bilanich drew a profound leadership lesson from an 1879 address to the West Point Corps of Cadets by General John McAllister Schofield, the superintendent of the Academy (Schofield also fought in the Civil War, was secretary of war under Presidents Johnson and Grant, and was commanding general of the United

States Army). Schofield told the cadets, "He who feels the respect which is due to others cannot fail to inspire in them regard for himself."

Bilanich translated General Schofield's nineteenth-century syntax into simple terms: "Treat everyone you meet with dignity and respect." He added, "If you want to build strong relationships with the important people in your life, respect them. Your respect will pay big dividends."[15]

By being continually mindful of the virtue of dignity, General John J. "Black Jack" Pershing demonstrated respect for himself, respect for his country, respect for other people, and respect for other cultures and religions. Through our dignified words and conduct, let's prove our own worthiness as we defend the human worth of the people around us.

6

DISCIPLINE

EXCELLENCE IS A HABIT

Today's United States Military Academy at West Point is a reflection of the personality of Sylvanus Thayer. Though the Academy was founded by President Thomas Jefferson, it is Thayer who is known as "the father of the Military Academy." Thayer rescued an Academy that was rapidly sliding toward chaos and disorder, and he instituted the educational standards and military discipline that are still followed at West Point to this day.

Sylvanus Thayer, West Point class of 1808, was born in 1785 in Braintree, Massachusetts. As a boy, he was fascinated by military life, and one of his favorite pastimes was talking to Revolutionary War veterans about their exploits. Napoleon Bonaparte was a special hobby of his, and he read everything he could about Napoleon's campaigns and tactics.

Thayer attended Dartmouth College, graduating in 1807 at the top of his class. He was making plans to give the valedictory address at the Dartmouth commencement exercises when he received word that President Thomas Jefferson had granted him an appointment to the Military Academy at West Point. The Academy had opened five years earlier on July 4, 1802. Thayer had been recommended to President Jefferson by General Benjamin Pierce, who was a friend of Thayer's family and a veteran of the American Revolution (he was also the father of a future president of the United States, Franklin Pierce).

Though West Point was, in theory, a four-year institution, standards were lax and cadets were graduated at the discretion of the instructors. Thayer's rigorous Dartmouth education had prepared him so well that he breezed through his coursework at the Academy in a single year. His instructors felt they had taught him all they could (he was already more proficient in most subjects than his teachers), and he graduated in 1808. Upon graduation, he received a commission as a second lieutenant in the Army Corps of Engineers. The first assignment for the twenty-three-year-old Lieutenant Thayer was to oversee the construction of Fort Warren in Boston Harbor.

Thayer served in the War of 1812 (which was fought against the British from 1812 to 1815). By this time, he was a captain in the Corps of Engineers. He fought in the Combat of Chateaugay River in 1813 and was in charge of the defense of the fortifications at the port of Norfolk, Virginia, in 1814. The British failed to capture Norfolk. As a reward for Thayer's effective leadership and meritorious conduct, the army gave him a brevet promotion to major.

The war exposed many weaknesses in the structure and discipline of America's armed forces. Thayer was appalled at the poor performance of army officers and the shocking unreadiness of

American troops. One factor, he believed, was the substandard education and training offered at West Point. The West Point "library" was little more than a single bookshelf. Leadership at the Academy was inept, and discipline at the Academy was practically nonexistent. Thayer had developed an excellent reputation in the Corps of Engineers, and he had built a good rapport with Colonel Joseph Gardner Swift, the chief of engineers. Thayer and Swift had talked at length about the problems in the army and at West Point. When President James Madison asked Swift for the name of an officer to send to France to study war academies and purchase European military books for West Point, Swift recommended Thayer.

The army paid all his expenses and provided a $5,000 letter of credit for the purchase of books and equipment for West Point. Major Thayer, accompanied by Lieutenant Colonel William McRee, arrived in Europe in July 1815. Thayer remained in Europe for two years, studying at the French academy École Polytechnique in Palaiseau near Paris (founded as a school of science but converted to a military academy under Napoleon). During his time in France, Thayer purchased hundreds of books and shipped them back to West Point. He also visited an artillery school at Metz in northern France and the acclaimed military school at the University of France, founded by Thayer's hero, Napoleon (who, one month before Thayer's arrival, had suffered a humiliating defeat at Waterloo in present-day Belgium).

Meanwhile, newly elected president James Monroe, who had served as secretary of war and secretary of state in the Madison administration, was painfully aware that the Academy at West Point was badly mismanaged. Monroe had visited West Point and had seen for himself that the cadets were undisciplined and disrespectful. He knew that Superintendent Alden Partridge (mocked by cadets as "Old Pewt") was incompetent, dictatorial, and erratic. Partridge had graduated from West Point in 1804 and had joined the West Point faculty immediately afterward. He had been superintendent since 1814. By the summer of 1817, Partridge had never lived one day as a real soldier but had spent his entire military career as a West Point academician.

President Monroe decided that "Old Pewt" had to go. He also knew that Major Thayer had performed his task in Europe expertly and thoroughly, and the books Thayer had purchased for the West Point library were an invaluable addition. He believed Major Thayer was the logical replacement for Partridge. When the president offered him the position, thirty-one-year-old Sylvanus Thayer accepted without hesitation.

When Thayer arrived at the superintendent's office and presented President Monroe's orders, naming Thayer as the new superintendent, Partridge refused to accept his firing. The army had to arrest Partridge and remove him from the superintendent's office. Once Thayer took command of West Point, he began reshaping the Academy in his own disciplined image.

<hr />

Thayer was shocked to discover how much conditions at West Point had deteriorated in the nine years since he had graduated. The place seemed to be ruled by paranoia and anarchy. Alden Partridge had arrested several West Point instructors, accusing them of conspiring against him. Partridge himself was teaching their classes. Most of the cadets were AWOL, and only forty cadets could be found on campus.

Historian Stephen E. Ambrose explained how the self-discipline of the new Academy superintendent helped impose a tradition of strong discipline at the once-disorderly institution:

> Thayer's greatest contribution to the Academy was the system he created, but he was able to introduce that system only through the strength of his own character. The impression he made upon cadets, faculty, congressmen, and the public generally gave him the trust and support he needed in order to inaugurate his reforms.

His personal appearance was majestic. . . . He looked the ideal professional soldier. His habits added to the impression. . . . His punctuality was unfailing and legendary. He arrived in his office on the stroke of the bell, at dinner parties at the exact hour of the invitation, at meetings at the precise moment of the calling to order. The annual June examinations of the cadets, a part of Thayer's system, were held . . . at eight each morning. Thayer would arrive at the examination room when the bugle sounded. . . . At the stroke of the one o'clock bell, Thayer terminated the examination, often in the middle of a cadet's answer.[1]

The demanding academic environment at Dartmouth had shaped Thayer's views of what an institution of higher learning should be. He was also strongly influenced by the military academies he had visited in France. Recently promoted Colonel Thayer imposed a set of rigorous new policies, requirements, and rules, most of which are now cemented into West Point tradition.

Henceforth, all cadets would be treated fairly, without favoritism or prejudice. Cadets would be required to maintain their physical fitness or be discharged. A system of demerits was instituted, and troublemakers would no longer be tolerated. Thayer divided the cadets into four classes and reaffirmed West Point's purpose as a four-year institution. He established rigorous academic standards, a code of honor, and a mandatory summer encampment. He required all cadets to conform to a military dress and behavior code.

The strict new disciplinary regime at West Point was not popular with the cadets, and one of Thayer's first actions upon taking command at the Academy was to put down a cadet mutiny and court-martial the ringleaders. The cadets responded angrily, saying the new superintendent did not have the authority to put cadets on trial. Thayer contacted the secretary of war and asked for a ruling. Secretary of War John C. Calhoun consulted with Attorney General William Wirt, who rendered a lengthy and carefully reasoned decision, concluding, "The Corps at West Point form a part of the land forces of the United States, and have been constitutionally subjected, by Congress, to the rules and articles of war, and to trial by courts-martial."[2]

That ruling still stands, and West Point cadets remain subject to military discipline, including court-martial. Thayer's authority and his decisions had been upheld at the highest level. The mutinous ringleaders left school, the cadets returned to their studies, and Thayer continued to carry out the mandate given him by President Monroe: reform the Academy and impose discipline on the institution.

Thayer noticed that problems arose because some cadets came from rich families and some were very poor. The cadets with a lot of extra spending money got into more trouble with drinking and gambling, while the poor cadets often went without the necessities of life, such as winter coats and boots. Thayer established an eighteen-dollar monthly stipend for all cadets, and he required every cadet to live within his means. None were allowed to receive money from home. This way even cadets from wealthy families learned self-discipline.

Thayer recruited a faculty of distinguished instructors in science and engineering, making West Point the preeminent school for those subjects. He not only elevated the prestige of West Point but also set an example for other colleges and universities to emulate.

◆━◆◆◆━◆

Sylvanus Thayer was a disciplined man in every respect. He was physically fit. He was extremely disciplined in his attire and appearance. He was so punctual you could set your clock by him. But the most disciplined aspect of Sylvanus Thayer was undoubtedly his mind. His memory was like a computerized spreadsheet in which he had filed the name of every cadet, along with up-to-date information about each cadet's grades, demerits, and any debts he might owe to the Academy. West Point cadets marveled at his ability to keep all that information in his head. (While he did have an excellent memory, he also had a desk with hidden pigeonholes in which he kept notes he could secretly consult when meeting with cadets in his office.)

The discipline imposed by Thayer was strict but impartial and fair. On one occasion, he attended a dinner party in Garrison, across the Hudson River from the Academy. During the party, Thayer encountered a cadet who was AWOL. Thayer was formally courteous to the cadet, who obviously did not expect the superintendent to be among the guests. After a few minutes of polite but uncomfortable conversation, the cadet excused himself and hurried back to West Point, fully expecting a richly deserved punishment to follow. But Thayer took no action against the delinquent cadet. Instead, he punished the hapless officer who was supposed to make certain the cadets were in their quarters.

Some cadets were not cut out to be soldiers. The most famous West Point dropout during Colonel Thayer's tenure was a young Edgar Allan Poe. Unlike most cadets, he had already served in the army, achieving the rank of sergeant major. At age twenty-two, he was over the legal age of admission and lied on his application to get in. Still, he had been a hard worker in the army, and his superiors spoke well of him. At his exams on January 4, 1831, he was academically near the top of his class, placing third in his class in French and seventeenth out of eighty-seven in mathematics. Poe easily could have been an outstanding West Point graduate, but he was undisciplined—a drinker, a gambler, and a black marketeer who operated a commissary out of his barracks room, selling liquor and other contraband items.

When Poe completed a book of poems in the fall of 1830, he showed them to Colonel Thayer, who was impressed with the poet-cadet's talent. Thayer encouraged Poe to publish his book, but Poe replied that he needed a list of subscribers (advance purchasers of the book) before a publisher would accept it for publication. Thayer suggested he seek subscribers among his fellow cadets.

One hundred thirty-nine cadets paid $1.25 each to fund his book, *Poems by Edgar A. Poe*, which he dedicated "To the U.S. Corps of Cadets."

At some point, as a reaction to a bitter dispute with his foster father, John Allan, Poe made up his mind to leave West Point in the worst possible way—via court-martial. Though he excelled in his exams on January 4, he stopped reporting for formations that entire month, stopped attending classes and chapel, and repeatedly flouted authority. He was court-martialed on February 8 for disobeying orders and neglecting his duty. Offering no defense, Poe was convicted and sentenced to dismissal. Colonel Thayer liked Poe, despite his recent insubordination, and arranged for leniency. He made Poe's dismissal effective March 6 so that the young man could receive another paycheck and settle his debts to the school.

Though technically on the Academy roster until March, Poe left West Point on February 19 with nothing but the change from his paycheck, a grand total of twenty-four cents. For the rest of his life, he always spoke kindly of Sylvanus Thayer.[3]

The inauguration of President Andrew Jackson in 1829 spelled trouble for West Point and Colonel Thayer. Previous presidents had always backed Thayer whenever he found it necessary to discipline and dismiss cadets. But Jackson believed in the political spoils system, the notion that politicians are entitled to do favors for friends and supporters. Quite a few wealthy donors to Andrew Jackson's campaign also had sons at West Point. When those privileged sons ran afoul of the West Point rules, their rich daddies would contact the president, and the president would reverse Thayer's decision. During his first two years in office, President Jackson reinstated sixteen cadets who had been dismissed from West Point.

Thayer believed in the chain of command, and he always obeyed the orders of his commander in chief. But he also wrote to President Jackson, informing him that it was becoming increasingly difficult for him to maintain discipline at the Academy, because politically well-connected cadets were shielded from consequences for their actions. The president ignored Thayer's pleas.

Finally, in 1832, Cadet H. Ariel Norris was court-martialed and dismissed from the Academy. President Jackson intervened and had young Norris reinstated. On his return, Norris bragged to his fellow cadets that his father's connection with the president meant he could do whatever he wanted at West Point, and Colonel Thayer couldn't do a thing about it. Norris was discipline proof.

To rub salt in Thayer's wound, Norris planted a hickory sapling in the middle of the Plain, West Point's parade field—a reference to Andrew Jackson's nickname, "Old Hickory." Thayer chose to ignore Norris and his insult. He wrote a letter to the secretary of war, explaining how the president's actions had destroyed discipline at the Academy, and he tendered his resignation.

When word of Thayer's resignation reached the cadets, young Norris was jubilant. He celebrated his victory over the superintendent by pelting a West Point officer with brass buttons, fired from a barracks window with a slingshot. Norris was court-martialed for assaulting the company officer—and dismissed from the Academy. This time the dismissal stuck. Norris was shocked to discover he was not discipline proof after all.

Colonel Thayer had demonstrated character and the virtue of self-discipline throughout his sixteen years commanding the Academy. He had transformed an institution on the brink of anarchy into one of the most prestigious institutions of higher learning in the world. Through the virtue of discipline, he turned West Point into a fortress of military instruction and leadership training that has proved invaluable to the defense and security of the United States of America.

When he announced his resignation, the faculty wanted to hold a testimonial dinner in his honor. Thayer was touched but refused to allow it. He was afraid it might be interpreted as criticism of President Jackson. One evening in July 1833, Thayer was walking with some West Point officers along the Hudson. He stopped at the steamboat dock, turned to his friends, and shook the hand of each one. Only when he turned and boarded a waiting riverboat did his friends realize he was saying his final good-bye.

Thayer continued to serve in the army for another quarter century. One of his great accomplishments after West Point was planning and overseeing the construction of fortifications around Boston Harbor. But he never visited West Point again.

Sylvanus Thayer retired on June 1, 1863, just a few days short of his seventy-eighth birthday. The following year President Abraham Lincoln nominated Thayer for an honorary promotion to brigadier general, retroactive to May 31, 1863, the day before his retirement. General Thayer lived quietly in his hometown of Braintree, Massachusetts, until his death at eighty-seven on September 7, 1872. He is buried at West Point Cemetery, and a statue of "the father of the Military Academy" stands on the Plain at West Point, a tribute to the man who brought honor and discipline to the Academy.

<hr />

In *The Story of Philosophy*, Will Durant observed, "We are what we repeatedly do. Excellence, then, is not an act but a habit."[4] Sylvanus Thayer repeatedly, consistently, habitually chose to be upright, ethical, and excellent in everything he did. He demonstrated excellence in his attire and his bearing. He demonstrated excellence in his highly disciplined mind and his physically disciplined body. He demonstrated excellence in always being punctual and dependable. He demonstrated excellence in setting forth rules of conduct and holding his cadets accountable, fairly and without favoritism.

The United States Military Academy at West Point became an institution of excellence because Sylvanus Thayer was a leader of excellence, a man of self-discipline. Success *is* the result of discipline, of repeatedly doing the things that lead to excellence. How, then, do we become self-disciplined in every aspect of our lives? How do we become the kind of people who choose the gym instead of the donut shop, a good book instead of a mind-numbing TV show, saving and investing instead of spending and consuming? How do we become the kind of people who consistently, habitually choose excellence instead of mediocrity?

Self-discipline is not a trait we are born with. It is a virtue we can practice and learn. We do not learn self-discipline overnight. We learn it over a lifetime. Here are some suggestions for building the disciplines that produce a lifetime of excellence.

1. *Emulate Sylvanus Thayer by building good habits.* Practice being physically self-disciplined through consistent diet and exercise. Practice being self-disciplined in your schedule by always being on time. Practice making consistently ethical and moral choices in even the most minor matters. As you practice building good habits in *one* aspect of your life, you will find yourself becoming more consistent and self-disciplined in *every* aspect of your life.

2. *Define what you want to achieve.* Clarify your dreams and goals, and write them down. As you state clearly and specifically what you hope to achieve, the discipline you need to achieve those dreams and goals will come into focus. You will see the changes you need to make, the bad habits you need to shed, the good habits you need to build, and the disciplines you need to impose onto your daily life. Once you know where you want to go, it is easier to figure out how to get there.

3. *Whatever you dream of doing, start now—then finish what you start.* Our cravings, desires, and laziness are at war with our goals, aspirations, and dreams. Undisciplined people may dream of accomplishing big goals—someday. But their dreams are only daydreams and never come to anything. Self-disciplined people don't wait for someday. They start *now* and turn their dreams into reality.

If you have trouble getting started on your big dreams and goals, try breaking a big, intimidating goal into smaller, simpler steps. Discipline yourself to work every day on those steps, and in time you will reach your destination. Instead of trying to write a novel, focus on writing one chapter or even one page—and maintain that focus day after day without fail. Instead of trying to lose forty pounds, focus on disciplining yourself to lose a pound every week.

Don't wait until conditions are "just right." Don't wait until that mythical day when you have "more time." Now is the time to build habits of self-discipline.

4. *Flee temptation.* Many people flirt with temptation. They keep temptation handy so they can yield to it at a moment's notice. In the back of their minds, they are planning to surrender to temptation, even if they consciously deny it. Self-disciplined people put miles of distance between themselves and temptation. They don't put themselves at risk. They don't flirt with temptation. They flee it—repeatedly, habitually, without fail.

5. *If you fail, forgive yourself and get back on track.* Everybody fails, even the most disciplined people. Don't beat yourself up. If you have committed a moral failure, confess it to God and anyone who was affected, repent of it and ask for forgiveness, then go and sin no more. If you failed because of a simple error in judgment, admit you failed, learn the lessons of failure, then keep pressing on to success and excellence.

Ask yourself what you could have done better, how you might have kept temptation away or made a better choice. Plan to prevent future failures. Don't let emotions of guilt or anger keep you from building habits that lead to success. Get right back into your disciplined lifestyle—don't delay.

6. *Find role models and mentors to help you become self-disciplined.* What do you want to achieve? Who is the most high-achieving person you know? Interview that person and ask, "How did you achieve that goal? What advice can you give me? How did you become so focused and self-disciplined?" Don't be afraid to approach successful people and ask for advice. Most will be eager to share their wisdom.

You can also find role models by reading books about people who have accomplished great things. In 1934, Harry S. Truman, then the presiding judge of Jackson County, Missouri, talked about some of his heroes. The one trait his heroes all had in common was self-discipline. As a boy of nine or ten, he read a four-volume book called *Heroes of History*. By age twelve, he had read the Bible from cover to cover—twice. His heroes included Jesus of Nazareth, Moses, the selfless Roman leader Cincinnatus, the Carthaginian general Hannibal, Cyrus the Great of Persia, King Gustavus Aldolphus of Sweden, George Washington, Robert E. Lee, and Ulysses S. Grant. Truman said, "In reading the lives of great men, I found that the first victory won was over themselves. . . . Self-discipline with all of them came first."[5]

Find mentors, encouragers, and role models by joining a group of like-minded people who want to build good habits and self-discipline into their lives. Meet with them on a regular basis, share your struggles and successes with them, and ask them to hold you accountable for your behavior, habits, and progress. It might be an exercise group, a writers group, a recovery group, a prayer group, or another group of people who share your goals. Ask them to hold you accountable for building good habits.

7. *Commit yourself.* Tell yourself you won't quit, you won't give up. Don't let anything stand in your way. Don't compromise. Don't procrastinate. Don't let obstacles stop you or slow you down. Don't rationalize. Don't make excuses. Be committed. Stay focused. Strive for excellence in every aspect of your life.

Then repeat, repeat, repeat.

7

INTEGRITY

HONEST AND TRUE

Major Dwight D. Eisenhower spent five years in the Philippines, assisting General Douglas MacArthur in his effort to prepare the Filipino Army for independence. During that time, Eisenhower became well acquainted with Manuel Quezon, the president of the Philippines. Eisenhower left the Philippines in December 1939. Two years later, Imperial Japan invaded the Philippines, forcing American forces to retreat. President Quezon left his own country and lived in exile in the United States.

In early 1944, shortly before Eisenhower departed from Washington, DC, to take command of the Allied forces in Europe, the exiled Philippine president paid Eisenhower a visit at his War Department office. During their conversation, President Quezon presented Eisenhower with a check for a substantial amount of money. Though the amount was never publicly disclosed, historian Stephen E. Ambrose wrote that "it was probably more than $100,000."[1]

Eisenhower was dumbfounded. "What is this for?" he asked.

Quezon replied that it was an honorarium for the services Eisenhower had rendered to the Philippine people as General MacArthur's chief of staff in Manila. Quezon added that he had also brought a citation to accompany the honorarium. Such a gift was perfectly legal. After all, MacArthur himself had already accepted a check from Quezon in the amount of $500,000, and Quezon had given smaller amounts to officers on MacArthur's staff.

But Eisenhower refused the money. Though he was far from wealthy, he did not consider accepting it for even a moment. He told the exiled president that while the gift was legal, and Quezon's motives were noble, it might create misunderstandings. Eisenhower was going to Europe to direct the Allied war effort. If his acceptance of such a large financial gift compromised his public image, it might ruin his usefulness to the war effort.

Historian and leadership expert Alan Axelrod observed that Eisenhower "expressed a very advanced form of ethical understanding. First, he understood that legal behavior and ethical behavior are not one and the same. The fact is that ethical action is almost always legal, but legal action is not always ethical. Ethical behavior must meet a higher standard than legal behavior. Second, he expressed his unwillingness to sacrifice larger, longer-term, and more important objectives for the sake of immediate gain, no matter how tempting."[2]

Quezon respected Eisenhower's integrity and his gracious but firm refusal of the honorarium. He then asked if he could issue a citation in Eisenhower's honor *without* a financial gift attached. Eisenhower replied that the citation would be of "more lasting value to me and my family than any amount of money."[3]

Dwight D. Eisenhower, West Point class of 1915, once expressed his view of integrity and leadership this way: "The supreme quality for leadership is unquestionably integrity. Without it, no real success is possible, no matter whether it is on a section gang, a football field, in an army, or in an office."[4] "Ike" Eisenhower served as supreme commander of the Allied forces in Europe, 1943–45; army chief of staff, 1945–48; president of Columbia University, 1948; and president of the United States, 1953–61. Eisenhower planned, organized, and gave the go-ahead for the D-Day landing at Normandy that was the turning point of World War II. He graduated sixty-first out of 164 cadets at West Point. Well liked by fellow cadets because of his daring, mischievous personality, he racked up more than his share of demerits and ranked ninety-fifth in conduct. He was honored at West Point with a cadet barracks named for him, and those who live in the Eisenhower Barracks will proudly tell you, "I live in Ike."

During his boyhood in Abilene, Kansas, Eisenhower aspired to a career in professional baseball. He once said, "When I was a small boy in Kansas, a friend of mine and I went fishing and as we sat there in the warmth of the summer afternoon on a river bank, we talked about what we wanted to do when we grew up. I told him that I wanted to be a real major league baseball player, a genuine professional like Honus Wagner. My friend said that he'd like to be President of the United States. Neither of us got our wish."[5]

The Eisenhower family was deeply religious and steeped in the Mennonite tradition of pacifism. Ike and his brothers were taught never to fight with neighborhood kids. Once young Ike was being chased down the street by a bully when Ike's father, David, arrived home from work. David called out to his son, "Ike, why do you let that boy run you around like that?"

"Because," Ike said, "if I fight him, you'll give me a whipping!"

"Ike, you chase that boy out of here!" And Ike did exactly that.[6] The Eisenhowers were Mennonites and pacifists, but pacifism had its limits.

Young Dwight Eisenhower excelled in spelling and arithmetic. There was a simple logic to both subjects. Words were spelled a certain way, as determined by the dictionary. Answers in arithmetic were either right or wrong—there were no gray areas.

But Eisenhower's favorite subject was history, especially military history. He devoted countless hours to reading history books, purely for enjoyment. In his 1967 book *At Ease: Stories I Tell to Friends*, Eisenhower recalled:

> My first reading love was ancient history. At an early age, I developed an interest in the human record and I became particularly fond of Greek and Roman accounts. These subjects were so engrossing that I frequently was guilty of neglecting all others. My mother's annoyance at this indifference to the mundane life of chores and assigned homework grew until, despite her reverence for books, she took my volumes of history away and locked them in a closet.
>
> This had the desired effect for a while. I suppose I gave a little more attention to arithmetic, spelling, and geography. But one day, I found the key to that closet. Whenever mother went to town to shop or was out working in her flower garden, I would sneak out the books.[7]

The Eisenhower family library contained many history books. The heroes young Dwight admired most were Hannibal, the military commander of Carthage, and George Washington, who won the Revolutionary War.

In his late teens, Eisenhower was the president of the Abilene High School Athletic Association and played center field on the baseball team. His brother Edgar played first base. At West Point, Eisenhower played junior varsity baseball (Omar Bradley was his teammate). When Eisenhower tried out for the Academy's varsity baseball team, he failed to make the cut. He recalled, "Not making the baseball team at West Point was one of the greatest disappointments of my life, maybe my greatest."[8]

Eisenhower graduated from Abilene High School in 1909. He and his brother Edgar worked out a plan to put each other through school. Edgar went to college first, while Dwight worked as a night supervisor at the local creamery.

In September 1910, Dwight learned that an examination would be offered for applicants to West Point and Annapolis. He took the exam and won an appointment to West Point. Though his parents were unhappy with his decision to become a soldier, they saw him off at the train station.

West Point was the realization of Eisenhower's boyhood fascination with the past. As a lover of history, he could imagine few greater joys than visiting places where Generals Grant, Lee, Sherman, and Custer had lived, studied, and, in some cases, were buried. Little did he know that he himself would become a part of history and that his graduating class would come to be known as "the class the stars fell on"—a reference not only to the "lucky stars" that seemed to bless this class with leadership potential but also to the star insignias reserved for generals. Of the 164 graduates of the class of 1915, fifty-nine achieved a rank of brigadier general or higher.

In 1916, after graduating from West Point, Eisenhower married Mamie Geneva Doud of Boone, Iowa. Ike and Mamie had two sons. Their first son, Doud, was born in 1917 and died at age three of scarlet fever. (Eisenhower rarely discussed the sorrow of losing his first son.) Their second son, John, who served in the army and retired a brigadier general, was the father of David Eisenhower, who married Richard Nixon's daughter Julie. Camp David, the presidential retreat in Maryland, is named after Dwight's father and grandson, both named David Eisenhower.

—◈—◈—

In 1917, Eisenhower was appointed commander of the tank training facility at Camp Meade, Maryland. Though he regretted remaining stateside during World War I, he contributed to future war efforts by devising new strategies for speed-oriented tank warfare. His superiors first resisted then adopted his ideas.

Eisenhower's vision for a rapid, mechanized invasion strategy has been validated in combat, from World War II through Operation Desert Storm.

In 1926, Major Dwight Eisenhower graduated from Command School at Fort Leavenworth, Kansas, number one out of a class of 275. In 1928, he again placed first in his class, this time at the Army War College.

Eisenhower was assigned as an aide to Army Chief of Staff General Douglas MacArthur in 1933. He would spend seven years under MacArthur, mostly in the Philippines. MacArthur wrote in a fitness report that Eisenhower was "the best officer in the Army. When the next war comes, he should go right to the top."[9] Despite that glowing assessment, MacArthur held Eisenhower back from advancing in his military career. Perhaps, at some point, MacArthur came to view Eisenhower as a potential rival. Much later, after Eisenhower became a five-star general, MacArthur said dismissively that Eisenhower was "the best secretary I ever had."[10]

Historian Matthew F. Holland suggested that Eisenhower's experiences under the brilliant but vain MacArthur probably prepared him well for his role during World War II, "when he had to work with such egotistical characters as Franklin D. Roosevelt, Winston Churchill, Charles de Gaulle, George S. Patton, and Bernard Montgomery."[11] Those experiences also served him well as president of the United States.

In 1939, Eisenhower returned to the United States to become commanding officer of the First Battalion, Fifteenth Infantry Regiment at Fort Lewis, Washington. Once he was no longer in MacArthur's shadow, Eisenhower advanced rapidly. In March 1941, he was promoted to colonel, and by October, he was a brigadier general. After the attack on Pearl Harbor, Army Chief of Staff George Marshall transferred Eisenhower to the War Plans Division in Washington, where he developed strategies for Allied invasions of Europe and Japan. Marshall's advancement of Eisenhower contrasts starkly with the way MacArthur roadblocked Eisenhower's career, as historian Stanley Weintraub observed:

> Eisenhower was an assistant to MacArthur—invisible, and painfully aware of going nowhere—and then deputy to Marshall, who rocketed him to responsibility and to prominence. In seven years with MacArthur, laboring in the arid peacetime vineyards, Eisenhower earned a promotion of one grade, from major to Lieutenant Colonel, changing the oak leaves on his collar from gold to silver. In seven months under Marshall . . . he earned a constellation of stars and a major command.[12]

In the spring of 1942, the army promoted Eisenhower to major general and named him head of the Operations Division of the War Department. General Marshall sent him to England to determine the condition of the European theater command. Finding chaos and disarray, Eisenhower returned with a gloomy assessment of American war readiness in Europe. In June 1942, Marshall sent Eisenhower back to London with the title Commanding General, European Theater of Operations. Marshall had passed over 366 more senior officers to put Eisenhower in charge. This speaks to Marshall's confidence in Eisenhower's leadership ability.

In November 1942, Eisenhower took command of a disorganized, mismanaged, multinational force in North Africa. He integrated armies from different nations into a coordinated force that launched successful invasions of Tunisia, Sicily, and Italy. He demonstrated such mastery of organization and strategy that, in December 1943, President Roosevelt named Eisenhower Supreme Allied Commander in Europe. Eisenhower had suddenly become the man uniquely responsible for the liberation of Western Europe.

+◆+◆+

Eisenhower was a "soldier's general" who enjoyed talking to the people he led. "I belonged with troops," he once said. "With them I was always happy."[13] In an address before the British Royal Military Academy, he said, "You must know every single one of your men. . . . You must be their leader, their father, their mentor."[14] Leaders earn the trust of their followers. Soldiers need to know their leaders genuinely care about them—and Eisenhower let his soldiers know.

When the troops boarded the transports that would take them to the beaches of Normandy, each soldier received a sheet of paper, "The Order of the Day," written and signed by General Eisenhower. It read in part:

> You are about to embark upon the Great Crusade, toward which we have striven these many months. The eyes of the world are upon you. The hopes and prayers of liberty-loving people everywhere march with you. . . .
>
> I have full confidence in your courage, devotion to duty, and skill in battle. We will accept nothing less than full Victory!
>
> Good luck! And let us beseech the blessing of Almighty God upon this great and noble undertaking.[15]

Historian Stephen E. Ambrose interviewed many soldiers who took part in the Normandy invasion. Many told how moved and inspired they were to receive "The Order of the Day" from Eisenhower. Ambrose recalled, "I cannot count the number of times I've gone into the den of a veteran of D-Day to do an interview and seen it framed and hanging in a prominent place."[16] Eisenhower's words reminded the troops what they were fighting for.

The D-Day invasion force consisted of 11,000 aircraft, 4,400 ships, and nearly 155,000 assault troops. The unknown variable in the plan was the weather. Eisenhower chose June 5, 1944, as the date for the landing, but a bad storm over the English Channel forced a postponement. Would the storm break and permit the invasion to go forward on June 6? If the Allies launched the invasion into the teeth of a raging storm, the assault would likely end in catastrophe.

The go-or-no-go decision would be Eisenhower's alone.

As the Allied armada sailed toward Normandy, General Eisenhower and other members of the Allied High Command gathered in the map room of Southwick House, near Portsmouth. They studied intelligence and weather reports. Eisenhower invited all opinions, and every leader in the room spoke his mind. Eisenhower listened carefully, sifting each opinion for wisdom and insight. The fate of nations hung on his decision, and time was running short. In a matter of minutes, it would be too late to recall the ships.

Finally, the room went silent, and Eisenhower sat still, thinking, thinking. Then he took a deep breath and said, "Okay, let's go."

Knowing the decision might end in disaster, Eisenhower had written a note that read, "Our landings have failed to gain a satisfactory foothold and I have withdrawn our troops. My decision to attack at this time and place was based upon the best information available. The troops, the air, and the Navy did all that bravery and devotion to duty could do. If any blame or fault attaches to the attempt, it is mine alone."[17]

Landing craft and amphibious tanks hit the beaches minutes after sunrise on June 6. Allied troops waded ashore facing a hailstorm of fire from German artillery and machine guns. By the time the Allies had captured some eighty square miles of French coastline, more than ten thousand soldiers were dead, wounded, or missing.

Operation Overload proved costly but successful. Eisenhower never had to deliver his note, taking the blame. Almost a year of fierce fighting lay ahead, but the Allied march to victory had begun.

On April 30, 1945, as the Soviet Army rolled through Berlin, Adolf Hitler took his own life. On May 7, German general Alfred Jodl drove to Eisenhower's headquarters in Rheims, France. He had come to sign an unconditional surrender. As a sign of contempt toward the German High Command, Eisenhower did not attend the signing. He sent his chief of staff, Walter Bedell Smith.[18]

Years later, Eisenhower's wife, Mamie, asked him where he found the courage to make that fateful D-Day decision—a decision that could have easily ended in catastrophe. He told her, "I had to. If I let anybody, any of my commanders, think that maybe things weren't going to work out, that I was afraid, they'd be afraid too. I didn't dare. I had to have the confidence. I had to make them believe that everything was going to work."[19]

◆━◆◆◆━◆

A year after the end of World War II, General Eisenhower and General MacArthur had dinner together at MacArthur's headquarters in Tokyo. MacArthur raised the subject of running for president of the United States. It was an ambition MacArthur had long harbored. Because MacArthur wanted so badly to become president, he assumed Eisenhower wanted it just as badly.

Eisenhower replied that he had no political ambitions. He subscribed to George Marshall's view that professional soldiers should not get involved in politics. MacArthur reached over, patronizingly patted Eisenhower on the knee, and said, "That's right, Ike. You go on like that and you'll get it for sure."[20]

Eisenhower was sincere. He wanted nothing to do with politics, but MacArthur didn't believe him. How could he? MacArthur wanted the presidency so much he could taste it. Certainly a leader of Eisenhower's caliber *must* have ambitions for the White House, right? But Eisenhower did not want the job. The first suggestion that Eisenhower should run for president came even before World War II ended, when historian Douglas Southall Freeman told him he should consider running for public office. Eisenhower responded instantly and vehemently, "God forbid!" After the war, both the Republicans and the Democrats approached him, offering a range of inducements if he would be their nominee. Eisenhower turned them down and accepted a position as president of Columbia University.

MacArthur and Eisenhower looked at leadership through opposite ends of the telescope. For MacArthur, leadership was about greatness, being admired, and leaving his mark in the history books. For Eisenhower, leadership was about being a servant, sacrificing for his country, and maintaining his humility. Eisenhower's humble view of leadership was beyond MacArthur's comprehension.

Eisenhower was the opposite of the kind of flamboyant, ego-driven leader MacArthur exemplified. Eisenhower led by careful planning, inspiring communication, spending time with the troops, and building trust. And the way he built trust as a leader was through his character—his integrity, sincerity, and honesty.

Much like George Washington and Ulysses S. Grant, Dwight D. Eisenhower was a brilliant strategist and a dedicated soldier who hated war and loved his troops. And like Washington and Grant, Eisenhower was a general who went on to become president, not out of ego and ambition but out of a sense of duty.

Eisenhower was finally persuaded to run as a Republican in 1952, feeling he had to block the nomination of Republican senator Robert A. Taft of Ohio. Eisenhower feared that Taft's noninterventionist foreign policy views, and especially his opposition to NATO, would play right into the Soviets' expansionist plans. Had Taft not thrown his hat in the ring, Eisenhower would not have run. Eisenhower narrowly defeated Taft in the Republican primary and went on to win the general election in a landslide, defeating Democratic candidate Adlai Stevenson II.

As president, Eisenhower maintained a balanced federal budget and an economy that elevated the standard of living of most Americans. He expanded Social Security coverage and proposed the interstate highway system. He desegregated the military and sent in the US Army to desegregate the public schools of Arkansas, as the Supreme Court ordered. He presided over eight years of American peace and prosperity. Before leaving office, he warned against the "military-industrial complex"—the greedy alliance between the military establishment and the arms industry, which can push the nation into wars for corporate profit.

Stephen E. Ambrose observed, "Scrupulous honesty was an integral part of Eisenhower's character. . . . He saw and experienced the payoff for trust. He knew that telling the truth was the only way to deal effectively with the problems."[21] And John W. Malsberger, in his book *The General and the Politician*, observed:

> Those who served with him during his long military career were invariably struck by how he exemplified . . . West Point values. British Admiral Sir Andrew Cunningham, who saw Ike regularly in action as the supreme commander of allied forces in Europe during World War II, found him to be "completely sincere, straightforward and very modest . . . always with a rather naïve wonder at attaining the high position in which he found himself." A French official during World War II similarly complemented Eisenhower on his great honesty. "I have found that you will not lie or evade in dealings with us, even when it appears you could easily do so."[22]

Eisenhower's eight years as president are remarkable for being free of any hint of scandal or impropriety. Malsberger attributed the squeaky-clean Eisenhower era to the president's own personal character and integrity:

> Eisenhower's . . . refusal to "play politics with the defense budget" or to "auction off the presidency," all grew out of his personal honor and integrity. He believed it was simply wrong for the chief executive to place the self-interest of any political candidate ahead of the general welfare of the nation. After all, he had agreed to seek the presidency in part to restore honor to the office that he believed had been so badly damaged by the intensely partisan actions of Franklin Roosevelt and Harry Truman.[23]

Eisenhower was reelected in 1956—another landslide. His victorious leadership in Europe during World War II undoubtedly fueled his political popularity. But his war record was only one facet of his popularity. Even more important was his reputation as a leader who could be trusted. One of Eisenhower's close friends was Paul G. Hoffman, the first administrator of the Marshall Plan (General George Marshall's plan to rebuild postwar Europe). When Eisenhower was running for president in 1952, Hoffman wrote to him, "One of your great appeals is your total integrity."[24]

When Eisenhower ran for president in 1952, his campaign's advertising agency, Batten, Barton, Durstine & Osborn, had one of the easiest selling jobs in history. When the agency crafted a fund-raising appeal aimed at Republican women, they built it around Eisenhower's reputation as a leader of integrity. "If General Eisenhower could go personally into every home in the United States, he would be elected overwhelmingly. His charm, his integrity, and his forthrightness are almost irresistible."[25] Eisenhower's campaign slogan, "I like Ike," was coined by Republican marketing expert Peter G. Peterson after market research showed that voters were far more energized by the trust they felt in Eisenhower's character than by any discussion of the issues.

People liked Ike because they admired his character.

———◆◈◆◈◆———

One accusation against Eisenhower's character needs to be addressed: the claim he had an affair with his Irish-born secretary, Kay Summersby, while serving as commander of the Allied forces in Europe. Many popular writers treat this claim as historical fact, while most responsible historians treat it as fiction. The claim seems to have originated with the book *Plain Speaking: An Oral Biography of Harry S. Truman* by Merle Miller, who interviewed Truman in 1962. Miller quoted Truman as claiming that Eisenhower had written to General George Marshall about his intentions to divorce Mamie and marry his secretary. Miller also quoted Truman as claiming he had the letters in his White House files but destroyed them.

Truman biographer Robert H. Ferrell went to the Truman Library in Missouri and listened to all the Truman interview tapes

Merle Miller used as the basis for his book. Ferrell stated, "There is no Truman conversation, nothing, about Kay Summersby. The tapes do not support the book's text—not by any means."[26] In fact, Ferrell said that *Plain Speaking* is riddled with Truman "quotes" that Miller seems to have invented to spice up the book. Miller waited until 1974—five years after Eisenhower's death, two years after Truman's death, and twelve years after conducting the interviews—to publish *Plain Speaking*. Dead people can't sue for libel or object to being misquoted.

Kay Summersby wrote a memoir in 1948, *Eisenhower Was My Boss*, which made no mention of an affair. A second book was published in 1975 in Kay Summersby's name, *Past Forgetting: My Love Affair with Dwight D. Eisenhower*. However, Kay Summersby was dying of cancer at the time. The book was ghostwritten by novelist Barbara Wyden. *Past Forgetting* was published after Summersby's death, and responsible historians give it little credence.

Both *Plain Speaking* and *Past Forgetting* continue to be quoted to this day. It is a tragic fact of life that people can say anything about great men and women—once they are dead. Reputations can be tarnished, history can be cast in doubt, and young people can be deprived of heroes and role models. The dead can't defend themselves. We, the living, owe it to the dead to check the facts and correct the record whenever lies are spread about them. It is a matter of our own integrity.

◆━◆━◆

A leader does not simply give orders. Great leaders must give the *right* orders, make the *right* decisions, take the *right* actions, and inspire and motivate their followers. That is why great leaders need good character. Their decisions and actions need to be rooted in traits of courage, honesty, and integrity. Leadership is based on trust, and people trust leaders of proven integrity.

We build our integrity moment by moment, year after year, by making moral decisions and speaking the truth. We strengthen our integrity by repeatedly doing the right thing, even when we don't have to, even when no one is watching.

The English word *integrity* comes from the Latin word *integer*, which means "whole" or "complete." In mathematics, an integer is a number without any fractional part. In the same way, a person of integrity is whole and complete—not divided or compartmentalized. A person of integrity will be the same person in public and in private. The inner reality will match the outward reputation.

Years ago, I researched a book on legendary UCLA basketball coach John Wooden. I interviewed one of his former student managers, who told me, "Here's the deal with John Wooden. The John Wooden on the practice floor was the same John Wooden in the locker room, and the John Wooden in the locker room was the same John Wooden on the campus at UCLA, and the John Wooden on the campus was the same John Wooden at home. He didn't change from place to place and situation to situation. There was an absolute consistency and integrity to his life."

How do you safeguard your integrity? I suggest "the firewall approach." Your car has a firewall between the engine and the passenger compartment. You hope you never need it—but if your engine catches fire, you'll be glad there's a firewall in place.

Your personal firewall protects you from getting burned by temptation. If you maintain certain "firewall" rules in your life, your integrity will be safe and secure. If you maintain a personal rule not to even take home a paperclip that belongs to your employer, you'll never get caught embezzling. And if you make a rule to never be in a compromising situation with someone of the opposite sex, you'll never have to explain to your spouse why you broke your marriage vows.

Don't think you can flirt with temptation and get away with it. Maintain *absolute* integrity. *Always* tell the truth. *Always* keep your promises. *Always* flee from temptation. Keep your moral firewall strong and impenetrable, and your integrity will never get scorched.

Integrity is more than mere honesty. It is being true to *all* your values, *all* your virtues, *all* your beliefs, in *every* situation of life. Young Eisenhower learned this lesson the hard way as a West Point cadet. He was raised by his parents to be a gentleman in the truest sense of the word—a *man* who is *gentle* toward others. As a third-class cadet (that is, a cadet in his third year at the Academy), Eisenhower was expected to take part in Beast Barracks—the six weeks of cadet basic training intended to turn civilians into cadets. Beast Barracks tradition required upperclassmen to "crawl" the "plebes" (haze the new cadets).

In the fall of 1912, Eisenhower was in a hallway when he saw a plebe dashing down the hall, carrying out some miserable chore on the orders of an upperclassman. Tradition required Eisenhower to stop the young cadet and make his life more miserable than it already was. So Eisenhower shouted, "Mr. Dumgard!"—the name for all lowly plebes.

The plebe stopped in his tracks.

"What was your PCS?" Eisenhower asked. The term meant "previous condition of servitude." Then he added sarcastically, "You look like a barber."

The plebe lowered his eyes and said, "I was a barber, sir."

Eisenhower turned away and went to his room. He told his roommate, "I'm never going to crawl another plebe as long as I live. As a matter of fact, they'll have to run over and knock me out of the company street before I'll make any attempt again. I've just done something that was stupid and unforgivable. I managed to make a man ashamed of the work he did to earn a living."[27]

And, true to his word, Eisenhower never engaged in hazing again. Mistreating the plebes was a West Point tradition, but Eisenhower realized that to do so would violate his character. When a demeaning tradition came in conflict with an essential West Point virtue, Eisenhower held fast to the virtue. He guarded his integrity.

8

LOYALTY

HE KNEW THEIR NAMES

General Matthew Bunker Ridgway, West Point class of 1917, had a habit of wearing a hand grenade on one shoulder strap of his jacket and a first-aid kit on the other. When asked if this was a form of showmanship, like General Patton's pearl-handled pistols, Ridgway said no. In wartime, he explained, soldiers sometimes found themselves cornered and were able to blast their way out with a grenade. He believed in being ready for any emergency, at any time.

Matthew Ridgway was the son of Colonel Thomas Ridgway, a West Point graduate and artilleryman. Matthew was born on March 3, 1895, and lived on various military bases throughout his childhood. Though his father never pushed him toward a military career, Matthew

Ridgway chose West Point because he wanted to make his father proud. He took the West Point entrance exam in May 1912 but failed the geometry section. He went home, studied math day and night for weeks, then retook the exam and passed with a 96 percent in geometry and algebra.

At West Point, he formed friendships that lasted throughout his life. He also suffered an injury that nearly ended his military career. He attempted to jump a hurdle on horseback but was thrown from the horse. He struck the wooden crossbar of the hurdle with his spine and landed on the ground in excruciating pain. He did not report the accident or seek medical attention for fear he might be medically discharged from West Point. The pain of that injury plagued him for the rest of his life.

During his first year at West Point, he developed a skill that would serve him well during World War II and the Korean War: the ability to memorize names. By the end of his first year, he knew every cadet at the Academy by name—all 750 of them.

He graduated around the middle of his class, fifty-sixth out of a class of 139 cadets. His class graduated just two weeks after the United States entered World War I. Ridgway wanted to be in the artillery like his father, and he hoped to go to France and see action. After spending a few months in Texas in the infantry, he was assigned to West Point as a Spanish language instructor and athletics manager. He recalled his disappointment:

> To me this was the death knell of my military career. The last great war the world would ever see was drawing to an end and there would never be another. Once the Hun was beaten, the world would live in peace throughout my lifetime. And the soldier who had had no share in this great victory of good over evil would be ruined.[1]

Of course, there would be more wars for Matthew Ridgway to fight. Unfortunately, World War I, known as "the war to end all wars," did not live up to its billing.

In 1925, Ridgway completed a course of officer's training at Fort Benning, Georgia, then took command of a company in the Fifteenth Infantry in Tsientsin, China. In 1927, his fluency in Spanish took him to Central America as part of the US mission to Nicaragua, helping to supervise free elections. In 1930, he became a military advisor to the governor general of the Philippines. In 1937, he completed a two-year course at the army's Command and General Staff School at Fort Leavenworth, Kansas. Promoted to major, he was mentored by Brigadier General George C. Marshall, a sign that the army recognized his leadership potential.

On September 1, 1939, Hitler invaded Poland, igniting World War II in Europe. Later that month, Ridgway joined the War Plans Division of the War Department in Washington, DC. In August 1942, he was promoted to brigadier general and assigned to command the new Eighty-Second Infantry Division. When the army converted the Eighty-Second into an airborne division, Ridgway earned his paratrooper wings and remained in command.

In early 1943, Major General Ridgway was the chief planner of the army's first major nighttime airborne operation on the island of Sicily. The army launched the invasion on July 10 and continued to send infantrymen in by parachute and glider over the next few days. During one disastrous parachute drop on the night of July 11, confusion and miscommunication reigned. Allied antiaircraft gunners mistook Allied transport planes for Axis bombers. Many Allied planes were shot down by friendly fire. Others scattered to escape the flak. Many paratroopers were killed or landed far from their drop zones.

Ridgway had to report to General George S. Patton, commander of the Seventh Army, that he had contact with fewer than four hundred of the more than fifty-three hundred paratroopers who had jumped into Sicily that night. Though Ridgway later established command of his forces, he never forgot the anguish and uncertainty of that night.

The mission to take Sicily was ultimately successful. By the end of July, the Allies had taken control of the island. The Eighty-Second Airborne had paid a heavy toll, losing more than a dozen transport planes and many paratroopers. Ridgway was determined to learn the lessons of that mission.

———————— ◆━◆━◆ ————————

Matthew Ridgway was fiercely loyal to his troops and devoted to their welfare. He once observed, "A commander must have far more concern for the welfare of his men than he has for his own safety. . . . All lives are equal on the battlefield, and a dead rifleman is as great a loss in the sight of God as a dead general. The dignity which attaches to the individual is the basis of Western civilization, and that fact should be remembered by every commander, platoon, or army."[2] He backed those words with action again and again during World War II and the Korean War. After his retirement, he vehemently opposed the wasteful losses of American soldiers in Vietnam.

Twice, as Allied war planners prepared to invade the Italian mainland, Ridgway saw disaster in the making. At considerable risk to his own career, he argued hard against both of those proposed operations.

The first involved a plan to send the Eighty-Second Airborne across the Volturno River to neutralize German artillery on the high hills beyond. Ridgway pored over contour maps and intelligence reports and discovered that his troops would be jumping into a flat, open plain between the river and the German-infested heights. The enemy would literally have the high ground from which to shoot down on his exposed troops. The plan was madness, and he told his superiors that if the plan went forward, the lives of many good soldiers would be thrown away. Fortunately, the planners heeded his warnings and called off the assault.

The second operation was even more ill-conceived than the first—and harder for Ridgway to stop. Code-named Operation

Giant II, the plan called for an airborne *coup de main*, a swift attack using speed and surprise to achieve victory with a sudden blow. The Italian government had secretly agreed on September 3, 1943, to an armistice with the Allies, effective September 9. The agreement stipulated that the Allies would defend the Italian government and royal family from retribution by the German occupation. The Allied plan was to drop one regiment of Ridgway's Eighty-Second Airborne Division on the northwest outskirts of Rome to support four Italian divisions in taking control of the Italian capital. As Ridgway studied the plan, he was aghast. Numerous unlikely conditions had to come together for the plan to work.

First, the paratrooper transports had to fly to Rome without fighter escorts (Rome was beyond fighter range). There was an excellent chance the paratroopers would be annihilated before they reached their target.

Second, six elite German divisions around Rome had to be caught completely off-guard. With so many unreliable Italian officials aware of the operation, there was almost no chance the Germans would not be tipped off.

Third, the paratroopers would arrive with few provisions and limited ammunition and would have to rely on the Italians for supplies and transportation—an iffy proposition at best.

Fourth, British field marshal Harold Alexander, the senior Allied officer in command, had promised Ridgway that ground troops would reinforce the paratroopers within three to five days to secure the liberation of Rome—a promise Ridgway flatly disbelieved. (In fact, Allied ground forces did not reach Rome until *seven months* later.)

Fifth, the enthusiastic citizens of Rome were supposed to rise up against the Germans and welcome the Americans as liberators. One of the planners of the mission, General Walter Bedell Smith, told Ridgway that the people of Rome would drop "kettles, bricks, and hot water on the Germans in the streets."[3] Ridgway considered that wishful thinking.

Though General Ridgway accepted chain of command and would not have defied an order, he knew the mission was suicidal, and he was desperate to change the minds of his superiors. Ridgway repeatedly argued against the mission with Field Marshal Alexander, General Smith, and the rest of Allied command. Alexander refused to abort the mission. Instead, he offered a compromise. Ridgway could send an American spy to Rome to investigate conditions on the ground.

General Ridgway's artillery officer, Brigadier General Maxwell Taylor, volunteered to go to Rome for a secret meeting with Italy's acting prime minister, Field Marshal Pietro Badoglio. If Taylor found the Italians could not keep their end of the bargain, he was to transmit a radio message containing the code word "innocuous."

General Ridgway waited in Sicily, painfully aware that time was growing short as the September 9 deadline loomed. A man of deep faith, Ridgway prayed that the mission would be aborted. "In such moments," he later wrote, "there has always been great comfort in the story of the anguish of Our Lord in the Garden of Gethsemane. And in all humbleness, without in any way seeking to compare His trials to mine, I have felt that if He could face with calmness of soul the great suffering He knew was to be His fate, then I surely could endure any lesser ordeal of the flesh or spirit that might be awaiting me."[4]

In the last few hours before the planes were to take off, Ridgway went to the division chaplain and asked him to walk with him. They went out in the countryside, praying and talking together. When they returned, Ridgway's anxiety about the mission was gone. He was at peace.

Maxwell Taylor arrived in Rome, disguised as a captured American airman, and met with Badoglio. He was thunderstruck by what the Italian leader told him. The Germans knew all about the planned invasion and had massed their forces around Rome. The Eighty-Second Airborne would be flying into a trap. Taylor got to a radio and transmitted messages over multiple channels, calling for the operation to be aborted. By the time the message reached the Eighty-Second Airborne, sixty-two transport planes were on the runways, carrying thousands of paratroopers, engines revving, preparing to take to the skies.

When General Ridgway heard that the mission had been called off, he sat down and wept tears of joy and relief. He later said that he was prouder of the one mission he helped to abort than he was of all the other missions he successfully completed. He knew those men would have flown off to certain death or capture. Through loyalty and persistence, he had saved them.

In May 1944, General Ridgway was in England, preparing his Eighty-Second Airborne Division for the D-Day invasion of Normandy. He had his mind made up to do something generals simply did not do. He was going to parachute into Normandy with his men. Allied command recommended he fly into Normandy with his division staff once the beachhead was secured. But Ridgway wouldn't be talked out of it. Though he had never jumped into combat, he had parachuted enough that he was confident about going in with his soldiers.

In the predawn hours of June 6, 1944, General Matthew Ridgway jumped out of a transport plane over northern France and landed in a pasture. By the dim moonlight, he saw something moving. Hoping it was one of his own men, he called out the challenge code word "flash." A friendly soldier would answer, "Thunder!" But the shape in the pasture answered, "Mooo!" It was a cow—and Ridgway was relieved. If there was a cow in the pasture, then it wasn't a minefield.

He turned a nearby apple orchard into his command post and proceeded to make contact with as many soldiers as he could. The first friendly face he saw was that of his aide, Don Faith, who had jumped right behind him. At first light, he made contact with

Sergeant Casey, his bodyguard. Soon they could hear the crack of small-arms fire, near and far, from all directions.

Moving a quarter mile to the east, they came to the village of Sainte-Mère-Église, which the Germans had abandoned. Some of Ridgway's troops had already taken it over. In the village, General Ridgway discovered his artillery commander, Andy March, who had come in by glider and had landed in the top of a tree. He was bruised but not badly hurt and was eager to fight.

During Ridgway's first day in Normandy, he constantly moved from place to place, going wherever the fighting was hottest. After gathering as many paratroopers as he could find, he led an attack against a small German force that defended a causeway over the Merderet River. The Allies needed that causeway to cross deeper inland—and General Ridgway personally directed the fight, forcing the Germans to withdraw.

Throughout the day, Ridgway went from one firefight to another, directing and encouraging his battalion commanders as they took the fight to the German occupation force. From time to time, he would return to his command post at the apple orchard. A messenger always arrived within minutes to report a new hot spot. On and on he trudged.

At the end of his first day in Normandy, he slept in a ditch outside Sainte-Mère-Église, grabbing the first shut-eye he'd had in forty-eight hours. Through the night, German artillery shelled the village.

During his first thirty-six hours in Normandy, Ridgway had almost no contact with the vast majority of his paratroopers. During the drop, they had scattered like dandelion seeds over a wider area than had been planned. But in time, radio communication was restored, and Ridgway was able to direct the advance of his troops against the enemy.

Why did General Ridgway make the risky decision to parachute into Normandy with his men? His reply: "Loyalty to the unit must start at the top." Ridgway believed that battles were won by men who felt bonded to one another by intense loyalty. A soldier's confidence and courage were bolstered when he saw his commanding officer alongside him at the front, sharing the risks instead of waiting safely behind the lines. Matthew Ridgway was a soldier, and he believed he should be at the front as a matter of respect for "this brotherhood that exists between fighting men."[5]

Ridgway later recalled an incident that took place during the fighting in Normandy. He had stopped at a farmhouse where one of his staff officers lay on a stretcher, being treated by a medic. The man had been shot in the bridge of his nose. Ridgway was offering encouragement to the wounded officer when a soldier on the next stretcher spoke up.

"Still sticking your neck out, eh, General?" the man said with a grin.

It was said with respect and admiration. The wounded man recognized the general as a fellow soldier. Ridgway never forgot that remark because "it represented the affection one combat soldier feels for another who has endured the same trials he has endured. For men who have shared combat together forever afterward have a common bond, no matter what their difference in rank may be."[6]

General Ridgway played a key role in stopping the desperate German counteroffensive known as the Battle of the Bulge. As the German attacks increased in ferocity, Ridgway remained cool, calm, and confident. On Christmas Eve 1944, amid the worst days of the battle, Ridgway calmly told his formation commanders, "The situation is normal and completely satisfactory. The enemy has thrown in all his mobile reserves, and this is his last major offensive effort in this war. This Corps will halt that effort, then attack and smash him. . . . I want you to reflect that confidence to the subordinate commanders and staffs in all that you say and do."[7]

He was constantly in motion, hurrying to the thick of the fighting to give direction and encouragement to his troops. Sometimes soldiers would be on the front lines in a foxhole, exchanging fire with the enemy—then realize that General Ridgway had jumped into the foxhole with them and was scanning the battlefield with his field glasses.

General Ridgway was loyal to the men he led, and they repaid his loyalty with respect, admiration, and trust.

◆━◆━◆

In June 1950, North Korea invaded South Korea. In December of that year, General Ridgway took command of the Eighth Army in Korea. The war had been raging for more than six months, yet the army was still in tactical retreat from North Korean and Communist Chinese forces. Ridgway found the Eighth Army in disarray. Soldiers were huddled in the snow without winter clothing. Food supplies were short. Morale was practically nonexistent, in part because the commanders were headquartered in the rear, safe and warm, having little contact with their troops.

On Christmas Day 1950, Ridgway went to Tokyo to meet with General of the Army Douglas MacArthur, commander of the United Nations forces in Korea. Ridgway wanted to know how much latitude he had to shake up the Eighth Army and turn it into a fighting force. MacArthur replied, "Eighth Army is yours, Matt. Do what you think best."

Ridgway began by reorganizing the command structure—and by getting rid of officers who were not trying to win the war. He attended a briefing at I Corps headquarters and listened to officers discussing their defensive plans and evacuation contingencies. Finally, Ridgway asked to be briefed on I Corps's attack plans.

The corps operations officer replied, "Sir, we have no attack plans. We are withdrawing."

Ridgway sacked him on the spot, then brought in officers who were focused on attacking the enemy and winning the war.

He fired officers who were not taking care of their troops. He found new officers to take their places, gave them full authority to do their jobs and take the fight to the enemy—and he held them strictly accountable for the results. Officers who did not do their jobs were bounced out. Officers who performed well received commendations.

In late January 1951, a revitalized Eighth Army under the command of General Ridgway launched a massive counteroffensive. By March 20, the Allies had pushed the North Koreans and Communist Chinese out of the south and had reached the thirty-eighth parallel, the border between North and South Korea.

Ridgway's loyalty toward his troops was demonstrated by an incident that occurred soon after he took over as commander of the Eighth Army in Korea. He was standing on a snow-covered ridge looking down on a road where a platoon of marines trudged along. One marine with a heavy radio strapped to his back tripped and nearly fell. Ridgway saw that the laces on one of his boots were untied.

The commander of the Eighth Army leapt from that ridge, slid down the snowbank on his rear end, and came to a stop at the feet of the radioman. He knelt down in front of the marine and tied the man's boot laces. General Ridgway never thought it was beneath him to perform an act of service for an enlisted man— even a marine.

By inspiring trust and lifting the morale of American armed forces in Korea, he reversed the momentum of the Korean War and changed the American mind-set from a defeatist, defensive way of thinking to one of confident offense. General Omar Bradley called Ridgway's accomplishment in Korea "the greatest feat of personal leadership in the history of the Army."[8]

In April 1951, President Harry S. Truman relieved General Douglas MacArthur of command of the United Nations forces in Korea and placed General Ridgway in charge. Ridgway also inherited MacArthur's position as military governor of Japan, and he oversaw Japan's return to sovereignty and independence on April 28, 1952.

Throughout his career, Matthew Ridgway built a reputation as a battlefield commander who led through loyalty. He was intolerant of incompetent officers, and he insisted on placing only the most dedicated and effective leaders in command of his units, because his soldiers deserved the best.

Just as he had learned the names of all his fellow West Point cadets during his first year at the Academy, Ridgway made a point of learning the names of all the soldiers he led. He literally knew the names of thousands and thousands of soldiers under his command, and they were always amazed and awed when their commander called them by name. His soldiers respected him but did not fear him. Rather, they wanted to please him out of love for a fellow combat soldier. Ridgway never used profane language. He spoke to his troops in a gentlemanly manner, even when administering discipline or correction.

He was always in the hottest part of the battle, often striding upright through a combat zone as bullets whizzed about him and artillery shells exploded on every side. He took what many would think was an incredibly risky gamble by parachuting into Normandy with his troops. When asked why he was so fearless in battle, he said it was because of his Christian faith. He believed that God had appointed a time for him to die and that there was nothing he could do to lengthen his life by a single second, nor was there anything the enemy could do to take his life from him before God's appointed time. That belief made him fearless as he faced the enemy.

General Matthew B. Ridgway died in July 1993 of cardiac arrest at age ninety-eight in his home in Pittsburgh, Pennsylvania. He is buried at Arlington National Cemetery. Chairman of the Joint Chiefs of Staff General Colin Powell eulogized Ridgway, saying, "No soldier ever performed his duty better than this man. No soldier ever upheld his honor better than this man. No soldier ever loved his country more than this man did. Every American soldier owes a debt to this great man."[9]

General Ridgway earned the respect and trust of every soldier who served under him. He led them, he cared for them, he was loyal to them, and he knew their names.

⸻⸻ ◆◈◆ ⸻⸻

Loyalty is a core value of the United States Army. The army's definition of loyalty is "Bear true faith and allegiance to the US Constitution, the Army, your unit and other Soldiers. Bearing true faith and allegiance is a matter of believing in and devoting yourself to something or someone. A loyal Soldier is one who supports the leadership and stands up for fellow Soldiers. By wearing the uniform of the US Army you are expressing your loyalty. And by doing your share, you show your loyalty to your unit."[10]

Unfortunately, all too many people in leadership, whether in the military or in civilian life, see loyalty as a one-way street. They demand loyalty from the people they lead but feel no obligation to demonstrate loyalty in return. General Ridgway viewed loyalty as a core virtue of his own life, a quality he demonstrated to the people he led and served. He expressed his loyalty by sharing the danger of combat with his soldiers, by parachuting in the dark with his soldiers, by making sure his soldiers' lives were not wasted on ill-conceived missions, and even by knowing the names of his soldiers.

Loyalty is based on a commitment, not feelings. You can be loyal to a person you don't even like. You are loyal to your troops and you take care of them not because you have a personal fondness for them but because they are your troops and you are committed to them.

Always stand up for your people. Always have their backs. If they are attacked or criticized, defend them. Always take care of your troops. That is what loyalty demands of you. After you defend them in public, you may have to confront them in private. Standing up for your people does not mean letting them get away with wrong behavior or character flaws. Loyalty isn't about being popular; it is about doing what is ethically and morally best for your people.

Loyalty is closely allied with servanthood. Loyalty makes a person willing to get down on one knee to tie a boot lace. Loyalty is essential to team building, whether in the military, the business world, the religious world, the sports world, or anywhere else. Loyalty produces cohesion in your team. When your people know you are loyal to them, they will be empowered to work harder, persevere longer, and take bolder risks. Let me suggest a few ways to build loyalty in your team or within your organization.

1. *Mentor your people and help them advance in their careers.* Help them discover their talents and sharpen their skills. Show them you care about them and want them to succeed.

2. *Keep your office door open.* I learned this principle from the great baseball executive Bill Veeck. He didn't just keep his door open—he took it off the hinges to make sure his people knew they could talk to him at any time. People will sense your loyalty to them when they know you are available to them.

3. *Give credit to your people.* Praise them publicly for their efforts and accomplishments. Affirm them and let them know you appreciate them.

4. *Challenge your people and inspire them to greatness.* Don't let them settle for mediocrity. Encourage them and motivate them to achieve more than they think they are capable of. Show them you believe in them and you trust them to achieve great things.

5. *Jump into the foxhole with them.* Get out on the front lines with them. Roll up your sleeves and share the grunt work and risks with them. Earn their appreciation and gratitude by being there with them—and for them.

6. *Be real.* Talk to them, get to know them, share your values and beliefs with them, and share stories from your life that will help shape their understanding of who you are. Let them know you as a real person, not a figurehead. Be honest, be transparent, be authentic.

7. *Know their names.* Get to know your people, who they are, what they care about, what motivates them, what makes them tick. And the first step is to know their names. You will be amazed at what a difference it makes when you call your people by name.

General Matthew B. Ridgway did not merely live the West Point virtue of loyalty—he personified it. He was the gold standard of loyalty. His soldiers loved him and wanted to make him proud of them. They knew he cared for them.

He knew their names.

9

PERSEVERANCE

REFUSE TO QUIT

It is rare to have three *brothers* at West Point at the same time. But three *sisters*? That is unique. During the 2013–14 academic year, the Corps of Cadets included Alexandra Efaw (class of 2014), Anastasia Efaw (class of 2016), and Arianna Efaw (class of 2017). But as Anastasia said, these sisters were destined for the Academy because "West Point is in our DNA."

Their parents, Andy and Amy Efaw, met at the United States Military Academy at West Point and were married six months after graduating in 1989. Andy is a lawyer and a colonel in the army reserves; Amy is a homemaker and a writer. In addition to Alexandra, Anastasia, and Arianna, the Efaws have a son, Andrew Jr., and another daughter, Aimee—and they, too, plan to go to West Point.

Alexandra jokes that growing up in the Efaw family was like living under martial law, so they all felt right at home at West Point. If one of the Efaw kids broke one of the family rules, the punishment wasn't "You're grounded." It was "Drop and give me twenty." The push-ups had to be counted out loud and performed with military precision. Once the push-ups were completed, the individual would call out, "Permission to recover!" Recovering involved "popping off" or loudly confessing the infraction and promising not to commit it again (for example, "I will not hit my sister!"). Failing to "pop off" loudly and enthusiastically enough could result in a repeat of the punishment.

Andy and Amy also used clipboards for room inspections, as practiced at West Point. Each Efaw sibling had a clipboard with a checklist of "mission-essential tasks" that had to be performed daily for the room to pass inspection. This way each child knew exactly what the expectations were—and whether he or she had met them. The checklist included items such as "brush teeth" and "make the bed" and a space for the time the task was completed. "It eliminated the 'I forgot' excuse," Andy explained. In a household of two adults and five children, West Point traditions brought order to what could have been a chaotic situation.

The Efaw siblings were required to participate in a sport, do push-ups and sit-ups every day, and sometimes run with Dad. Andy would call cadences as they ran, and the kids would answer back—which would attract the stares of strangers. But the practice helped prepare the three Efaw sisters for West Point. They already knew the cadences used at the Academy, so West Point was almost like home.

The Efaw sisters were never pressured to attend the Academy, yet they couldn't imagine going to college anyplace else. With both parents, two uncles, and an aunt having graduated from the Academy, it was simply the place to go. Alexandria said that even when she found out that other schools existed, she still wanted to go to West Point.[1]

The three Efaw sisters were profiled in a 2014 *New York Times* piece titled "The Women of West Point." One fact that came through is that it takes a lot of perseverance to get through four years at West Point—and this is doubly true for female cadets.

Arianna Efaw encountered reactions ranging from skepticism to outright derision when she told fellow cadets she wanted a career in the infantry. "Whenever I tell people I want to go infantry, they laugh in my face," she said. When male cadets treated her ambitions with condescension, it fired up her motivation to prove them wrong. She added, "You want to be better than the guys to prove that you belong here."

The competition at West Point is intense, because everyone who makes it into West Point is the best of the best. "You get into West Point," Arianna reflected, "because you're good academically, you're a good leader, you're the team captain or whatever. Then you get here and realize that everybody's exactly like you, only better."

Though the competition is intense, West Point friendships are also intense. Fellow cadets become an indispensable resource for maintaining the virtue of perseverance through stressful times. "What I like most about West Point," said Anastasia, "is the relationships you make here because of what you go through and how stressful it is. A week is like a month in real life. . . . We have this unique experience that we're all sharing with each other."[2]

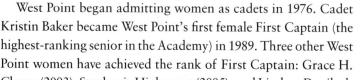

West Point began admitting women as cadets in 1976. Cadet Kristin Baker became West Point's first female First Captain (the highest-ranking senior in the Academy) in 1989. Three other West Point women have achieved the rank of First Captain: Grace H. Chung (2003), Stephanie Hightower (2005), and Lindsey Danilack (2013). On average, women make up about one-fifth of all new first-year cadets.

After making first captain, Lindsey Danilack from Montville Township, New Jersey, recalled her first year at West Point: "I knew I was going to need to step it up in the physical realm," she said. "But I never knew it was going to be as hard as it turned out to be. . . . I honestly cannot believe that I've made it this far. . . . In high school, one of my teachers actually told me that I would never get into West Point, that it was too hard."[3]

Danilack captained the women's track and field team, competing in several events, including the 400-meter hurdles. She said she accepts that she can't run as fast as the male two-milers at West Point, but she takes a back seat to no one as a leader. After all, hers is the 143rd name on the plaque listing past first captains at West Point. Other names include John J. Pershing and Douglas MacArthur. She was at the very top of the cadet chain of command and the leader of the entire West Point Corps of Cadets.

"We're all trying to accomplish very similar goals, regardless of gender," she concluded.[4] After graduating from West Point in 2013, she went to Fort Rucker, Alabama, to be trained as an Apache helicopter pilot. She has also parachuted from fixed-wing aircraft, rappelled out of helicopters, and worked at the Defense Intelligence Agency in Washington, DC.

———————◆◈◆———————

Emily Jazmin Tatum Perez, West Point class of 2005, entered the Academy in July 2001. After the terrorist attacks of September 11, 2001, she became part of the so-called class of 9/11 because the attacks occurred soon after the start of her freshman year. Born into a proud military family in Heidelberg, West Germany, of African American and Hispanic parents, Emily Perez was a top student and a talented musician in high school and at the Academy. On the track, she could outrun most male cadets.

A devout Christian, Perez was enthusiastically involved in her church and helped start an HIV/AIDS ministry there. (She was also a Red Cross HIV/AIDS educator.) She directed a gospel choir, read her Bible daily, and lived its teachings faithfully. Her pastor, Rev. Michael Bell of Peace Baptist Church in Washington, DC, called her "one of the most brilliant people I ever met . . . the consummate intellectual."[5]

After graduating from West Point in 2005 (in the top tenth of her class), Perez was commissioned as a second lieutenant in the 204th Support Battalion, Second Brigade, Fourth Infantry Division of the Army. Days before shipping out to Iraq, Lieutenant Perez flew halfway across the country to donate bone marrow to a stranger. She went to Iraq as a Medical Service Corps officer.

On September 12, 2006, Lieutenant Perez looked at a lieutenant who was supposed to lead a convoy through Al Kifl, a village on the Euphrates in southeastern Iraq. Something told her the lieutenant was not in shape to lead. She volunteered to lead the convoy herself and told the lieutenant he could take her place in back.

As the convoy passed through the village, an improvised explosive device detonated next to her vehicle. Perez, age twenty-three, died in the explosion. The translator in the seat next to her suffered traumatic amputation of both legs. Soldiers in the back of the vehicle received minor injuries.

Tiffany Martin, Emily Perez's West Point roommate, said she was always persevering in doing good for others. "She wanted to help young women," Martin said. "She wanted to help African-Americans." Emily's mother, Vicki Perez, agreed. "She would put her life on hold to take care of the needs of others," she said.[6]

She was the first soldier of "the class of 9/11" to die. There would be others.

◆━◆━◆

The night of September 11, 2001, while the horror of the terror attacks was still fresh, the cadets assembled on the Plain and heard a bugle sound "Taps." Each cadet had his or her own private thoughts on the meaning of that day when the homeland was attacked in lower Manhattan and at the Pentagon and when American heroes fought the attackers over the skies of Pennsylvania. But all the cadets together shared one inescapable thought:

America was going to war, and this class of West Point cadets would serve in wartime.

Emily Perez was one of the cadets who stood on the Plain at West Point that night. Another cadet in the assembly that night was Walter B. Jackson.

On September 27, 2006, Second Lieutenant Jackson was serving as a company fire support officer with Company A, Task Force First Battalion, Thirty-Sixth Infantry Regiment in Al Anbar Province, Iraq. During combat operations against insurgents, Lieutenant Jackson was trying to recover a disabled vehicle when heavy machine-gun fire erupted, wounding several soldiers. As he rushed to give aid to one of the wounded men, he was hit in the thigh.

He fell and was unconscious for a few moments. The shouts of his comrades and the rattle of machine-gun fire woke him. He picked up his weapon and returned fire, then went back to work on the wounded soldier. Once he had administered first aid, Jackson lifted the wounded man and began carrying him, though he was bleeding profusely from his own wound.

As he crossed the open ground toward safety, he was again hit by machine-gun fire. Persevering through the pain and loss of blood, he continued carrying his man until he had put a stone wall between himself and the enemy. Jackson's own wounds were life-threatening, yet he refused help until the other man was treated. Shot multiple times, he refused to stay down. He cared more for his friend's life than his own. He was selflessly brave and he relentlessly persevered, saving the life of his brother in arms.

After the battle, Jackson underwent more than a dozen surgeries to repair the damage inflicted on his body that day. During his recovery, he volunteered to intern with the Judge Advocate General's office.

For extraordinary heroism under fire, Lieutenant Jackson was awarded the Distinguished Service Cross, the second-highest honor (next to the Medal of Honor) the nation can bestow. He is only the seventh soldier to receive the Distinguished Service

Cross since the end of the Vietnam War. Jackson was also honored
with the Nininger Award (named for World War II hero Alexander Nininger, West Point class of 1941), given to West Point–
commissioned officers who have demonstrated heroism and bravery in battle.

In his Nininger Award acceptance speech on September 17,
2008, Walter B. Jackson (wearing the two silver bars of an army
captain), said:

> The Long Gray Line has historically produced soldiers of remark-
> able courage and valor—true combat leaders such as Grant, Mac-
> Arthur, Pershing, Eisenhower, and countless others. Whether you
> realize it or not, that includes each of you. Up until the time when I
> was wounded in action, I never really thought it might include me.
>
> The recognition I have received and continue to receive is simply
> overwhelming. The Distinguished Service Cross that I wear, and
> the honor of receiving the Nininger Award tonight are not so much
> for me personally, but I receive them as a tribute as a reminder of
> the heroism displayed by my classmates, Emily Perez, Phil Neel,
> Tom Martin, Jacob Fritz, Jon Edds, Neale Shank, and my room-
> mate Matt Ferrara—all who have made the ultimate sacrifice. . . .
>
> Focus on the mission, take care of your soldiers, and persevere.
> In the future you all will be called on to persevere through any
> adversity, whether it is physical pain or constant fatigue, mental
> stress or fear. Each of you at some point will face challenges that
> will shake the foundations of your character. When that day comes
> I know that you will do your duty with honor for your country. . . .
>
> West Point trains you. The Army will be—without a doubt—
> your proving ground.[7]

Who were these fallen heroes of the class of 9/11 that Captain
Jackson listed? We have already met Emily Perez. But there was
also Captain Matthew C. Ferrara, Jackson's West Point roommate.
Captain Ferrara was killed (with four other soldiers) on November
9, 2007, in an ambush in the village of Aranas in Kunar Province,

Afghanistan. Ferrara was posthumously awarded the Silver Star—not for his actions on the day he was killed but for his heroism three months earlier.

At the army's Ranch House Outpost at Aranas, on the morning of August 22, Matt Ferrara was awakened by the sound of gunfire and exploding rocket-propelled grenades. The outpost was under attack from all sides, and the enemy outnumbered the Americans three to one. Stepping outside his quarters, Ferrara quickly began deploying soldiers and directing mortar fire at the enemy.

Ferrara determined where the most effective enemy fire was coming from and called in air strikes on those positions, marking his own location with a bright orange signal panel. The signal panel was an excellent visual guide for the American A-10 attack aircraft, but it also shouted his location to the enemy. Insurgents came within ten yards of his position before the A-10s began to strafe. Heedless of the danger to himself, Ferrara continued to call in air strike targets until the enemy was dead or retreating.

His calm and precise assessment of the situation, his rapid decisions, his effective direction of close air support, and his courage and perseverance in the face of deadly fire for *three intense hours* of combat prevented the enemy from overrunning the Ranch House Outpost. Nearly a dozen enemy fighters were killed, including insurgent leader Hazrat Omar.

And then there was First Lieutenant Phillip Neel, who died on April 8, 2007, from wounds suffered when his unit was attacked by enemy forces using grenades. The twenty-seven-year-old infantry officer was leading a platoon near Balad in the Diyala Province, north of Baghdad. At about ten minutes after midnight on Easter Sunday morning, he suffered a serious leg wound, yet he continued to give orders to his soldiers. After the enemy was forced to retreat, Lieutenant Neel was airlifted by medevac helicopter, but he died at around two in the morning.

First Lieutenant Thomas Martin was an army ranger who never hesitated to volunteer for the toughest jobs. As a youth, he was always giving to his community; active in his church; and involved in 4-H, high school band, and Boy Scouts, achieving the rank of Eagle Scout. At West Point, he was on the parachute team and often performed aerial free-fall designs and formations in national competitions. His mother and father were both in the army and so was his fiancée, Captain Erika Noyes, a medevac helicopter pilot. Whenever he emailed his mother, Candy Martin, from Iraq, he always signed off, "I gotta go rid the world of evil." That is what he was doing in the final moments of his life on October 14, 2007, in Al Busayifi, Iraq, when insurgents attacked his unit with small-arms fire.

First Lieutenant Jacob N. Fritz from Nebraska was one of four US soldiers abducted during an ambush in Karbala, Iraq, on January 20, 2007. The soldiers were taken from their compound and later found dead, handcuffed together and executed near the southern Iraqi town of Mahawil.

First Lieutenant Jonathan W. Edds died on August 17, 2007, in Baghdad from wounds he suffered when an improvised explosive device detonated near his vehicle and insurgents attacked with small-arms fire. His wife, Laura, described him as an easygoing, fun-loving young man who was good at his job. He was patrolling Baghdad when he was attacked and killed.

First Lieutenant Neale M. Shank died on March 31, 2007, from injuries he suffered in Baghdad from a noncombat-related incident. Family and friends who knew him said he was a dedicated soldier with great integrity. Ironically, he had survived a tour of duty in some of the most dangerous areas of Iraq and had recently been moved to Baghdad, which was considered a much safer place to be. He told family members that he had been greatly affected by the sight of Iraqi children enduring incredible hardships and danger, and he wanted to help those kids have a better life.

These fallen heroes were part of the class of 9/11, the first class of cadets to be trained at West Point during the post-9/11 War on Terror. When they graduated from the Academy in May 2005, their class consisted of precisely 911 newly commissioned army officers, an eerie coincidence to be sure. Each in his or her own way demonstrated the core virtues of West Point, especially the virtue of perseverance.

———————— ♦━◆━♦ ————————

How do we build the West Point virtue of perseverance into our own lives and the lives of the people we lead? How do we apply it in our leadership roles, our military or civilian careers, and the challenges we face in life? Let me suggest some insights that arise from the lives of these West Point heroes.

1. *Learn to persevere longer through competition.* Surround yourself with people who challenge you to step up your game and be your best. The Efaw sisters thrive on competition, because competition makes us stronger, leaner, tougher, more resilient. Competition drives us to persevere and become champions and heroes.

2. *Lean on supportive friends.* Your friends are an indispensable resource for persevering through times of struggle and stress. Find people who are going through what you are going through, people who can relate to you, and you to them. Encourage each other, challenge each other, pray for each other, hold each other accountable, cheer each other on.

3. *Focus on your strengths, not your limitations.* Lindsey Danilack admitted she wasn't as fast as other cadets, but she was a strong leader. She focused on her strengths, not her limitations— and that is why her name is on a plaque along with Pershing and MacArthur.

4. *Replace negative self-talk with messages that empower you to persevere.* Replace "I can't go on" with "I can do this." If you are running a marathon, don't think about the finish line. Tell yourself, "I can run one more mile." Do this mile after mile, and you will get to the finish line. I know this strategy works, because I've used it to complete fifty-eight marathons.

If you are building a business or an organization and you are facing exhaustion and frustration, tell yourself, "I can do this for one more day." Keep telling yourself "one more day," day after day, and you will achieve your goal. I know this works because that is how I kept going when building the Orlando Magic out of little more than dreams and pixie dust. In 1986, I went weeks on end with very little sleep, giving speeches, meeting with civic leaders and investors, doing media interviews, and trying to sell season tickets for a team that might never exist. The Orlando Magic exists today because positive self-talk really does enable us to persevere through the tough times and achieve our goals.

5. *Get involved in athletics.* Physical exercise and physical competition help you develop grit and staying power. Athletic work is as much a mental exercise as it is a physical one, and the strength and stamina you build through physical activity are transferable to every other kind of challenge you face.

We grow physically, mentally, emotionally, morally, and spiritually stronger by subjecting ourselves to physical stress. We develop a stronger will to endure. Sports and exercise encourage us to persevere longer in every aspect of our lives.

6. *Accept challenges that intimidate you.* Don't settle for the path of least resistance. Take on goals, challenges, and dreams that scare you and demand more of you. The best way to find out what you are made of is to tackle a challenge that is too big for you—and see it through to completion. Push through the obstacles. Laugh at opposition. Keep going, going, going.

7. *Read stories about people who have achieved the "impossible."* Picture yourself in their place, facing seemingly insurmountable odds. How did they overcome obstacles and opposition? What kind of attitude did they adopt? What resources did they draw upon to find the will to win? Find role models of perseverance, identify with their struggles, and learn the lessons of their lives. If possible, write to them or visit them and ask them how they were able to persevere through their toughest challenges.

8. *Persevere for the people you care about.* Tell yourself, "I'm going to conquer this addiction or beat this cancer or lose this weight or overcome this career setback to set an example for my kids." If you commit yourself to being a role model of perseverance for the people who matter to you, you will find it hard to say, "I give up" or "I can't go on." Instead, you will say, "I've got to keep going. I've got to reach the finish line. The people I love are counting on me."

9. *Make a vow or a commitment to see a challenge through.* Political strategist Robert Strauss is quoted as saying, "Success is a little like wrestling a gorilla. You don't quit when you're tired—you quit when the gorilla is tired."[8] Commit yourself to the proposition that you will not quit no matter what, and you will be able to persevere.

The summer before I entered the ninth grade, I tried out for a sandlot baseball team. I made the cut, though I was the youngest player on the team. I was happy I had made it, but I wondered if I could perform at that level. As my mother and grandmother drove me to my first game, we talked about my prospects with the team.

At one point, I said, "Well, if it doesn't work out, I can always quit."

My grandmother whirled around and poked her finger in my chest. "You. Don't. Quit," she said, emphasizing each word. "Nobody in this family quits!"

Well, I got the message—and I didn't quit. That character-building moment has been the foundation for everything I have achieved in life, from running marathons to building a professional sports organization to beating cancer. God bless my grandmother. Thanks to her, I don't quit. And I have taught my nineteen kids the same lesson: nobody in this family quits.

10. *Just do it.* Don't think—act. Thinking stirs up doubts, and doubts are deadly to perseverance. Action puts an end to doubts. Vincent van Gogh put it this way in an 1883 letter to his brother Theo: "If you hear a voice within you saying, 'You are not a painter,'

then by all means paint, boy, and that voice will be silenced, but only by working. . . . One must undertake it with confidence."[9] Action is the key to perseverance and success.

11. *Live passionately*. Enthusiasm powers perseverance. Do what gives your life meaning and purpose, and you will never be tempted to give up. When you are mentally spent and physically exhausted, where do you find the will to go on? It comes from your passion to succeed and overcome.

When a soldier like Lieutenant Jackson keeps going, keeps tending to his wounded buddy, keeps carrying his comrade to safety even after being shot several times himself, where does he find the strength to persevere? He finds it in his passionate will to live, his passionate will to save his fellow soldier, his passionate will to go home to the people and the country he loves, his passionate determination to complete his mission.

Live passionately and persevere with enthusiasm.

12. *Pray for the power to persevere*. Ask God to energize your mind and body, to put steel in your spine, and to send your spirit soaring. Never give in. Never give up. Never quit. Live out the West Point virtue of perseverance. Finish strong.

——10——

RESPONSIBILITY

"NO EXCUSE, SIR!"

Mike Krzyzewski, West Point class of 1969, is the head men's basketball coach at Duke University. He has coached the Duke Blue Devils to five NCAA championships (only UCLA's John Wooden has won more, with ten) and twelve Final Fours. He also coached the USA men's basketball team to gold medals in the 2008, 2012, and 2016 Summer Olympics. He is widely known as Coach K. In his book *Leading with the Heart*, Krzyzewski talks about a crucial life lesson he learned in his first few weeks at West Point.

Arriving at the Academy in July 1965, Krzyzewski was looking forward to what the brochure called "Summer Orientation." He wasn't aware that the cadets called it by another name: Beast Barracks. During Beast Barracks, an incoming cadet ceases to be an individual human being and becomes a plebe. Krzyzewski quickly learned that when an upperclassman asks a question, there are only three acceptable answers a plebe can give: "Yes, sir," "No, sir," and "No excuse, sir."

Soon after his arrival, Krzyzewski and his roommate were walking across an open space when his roommate stepped in a puddle. A few drops of mud splashed onto Krzyzewski's mirror-polished shoes. They continued walking, then heard the sound every plebe dreads: "Halt!"

Two upperclassmen approached and looked them up and down. One said to Krzyzewski's roommate, "You're okay."

They looked at Krzyzewski, giving special attention to his name tag. "What's your name?"

Krzyzewski pronounced his last name for him.

"What kind of name is that?"

Krzyzewski said nothing.

"Your shoes are cruddy. You're a crudball. How did that happen?"

Standing at attention, Krzyzewski replied, "No excuse, sir."

"That's right! You have no excuse!" And the upperclassman proceeded to verbally abuse the poor plebe for the next few minutes. Then he wrote Krzyzewski up and gave him demerits for having mud on his shoes.

When Krzyzewski caught up with his roommate at the barracks, he was livid. "Look what you did to me!" he said, holding up the demerit slip.

After a few weeks of cadet basic training, however, Krzyzewski began to understand the meaning of the West Point virtues, especially the virtue of responsibility. His perspective gradually changed. He realized he had been wrong to blame his roommate. When his roommate accidentally splashed mud on his shoes, Krzyzewski had a choice. He could have gone back and cleaned his shoes, but he chose instead to ignore the mud. It wasn't Krzyzewski's fault his roommate stepped in that puddle, but Krzyzewski was still responsible to keep his shoes clean.

"I had no right to be mad at my roommate," Krzyzewski later reflected. "I should have been mad at myself. And later, when I understood the reality of the situation, I *was* angry with myself. That was a huge lesson for me."[1]

That lesson stuck with him and shaped his attitude toward coaching. He realized that no matter what happened, he was the coach, he was responsible, and he had no excuses. He taught that same virtue of responsibility to his players. Every player is responsible to do his job, and if he fails to meet his responsibility, he is letting his teammates down.

Whether on the basketball court or the battlefield, there is no time to have extended conversations about who is to blame for this or that foul-up. Every player, every soldier, must take personal responsibility. There can be no excuses, no shifting of blame. Everybody is responsible. If one player or one soldier fails, everybody suffers.

Krzyzewski learned another lesson in responsibility during Beast Barracks. There were thirty plebes in his platoon, three in each room of the barracks. The plebes were standing around outside the barracks in their fatigues when the squad leader showed up and ordered them to assemble in full dress uniform—*in two minutes.*

The plebes scrambled into their rooms, fumbled with their uniforms, and got in each other's way, each one trying to be the first out the door. A few plebes lined up in front of the barracks. Then a few more. Then the last few stragglers. Not one of them arrived within the specified two minutes.

The squad leader glared at the lineup of plebes. "Why are you late?"

"No excuse, sir!"

"If one of you is late, all of you are late. Do you understand? If you guys would work together, you might make it in two minutes."

Krzyzewski and his fellow plebes realized what the squad leader was teaching them. The plebes weren't working together.

Each man was working *by* himself *for* himself—and making everybody late.

So the plebes practiced working together. They came up with a system in which the roommates would help each other out of their fatigues and into their dress uniforms. Working together as a unit, they achieved the impossible. They reassembled in front of the barracks in less than two minutes.

After earning the squad leader's approval, they went back to their rooms, talking excitedly and high-fiving each other. "I get goosebumps when I think of it," Krzyzewski wrote. "We learned to depend on one another, which, in turn, made us better. . . . It was an add-on to personal responsibility. It was collective responsibility."[2]

That is how the West Point virtue of responsibility works. Every cadet must be personally and individually responsible. And all the cadets must be collectively responsible. One is responsible for all; all are responsible for one. When working together, with each cadet accepting full responsibility, there is no limit to what they can achieve together.

◆━◆◆◆━◆

General Douglas MacArthur graduated at the top of the West Point class of 1903. He was the son of Lieutenant General Arthur MacArthur Jr., who was awarded the Medal of Honor for heroism in the American Civil War. Douglas MacArthur was nominated for the Medal of Honor for conducting a daring reconnaissance mission during the 1914 US occupation of Veracruz, Mexico. He was nominated a second time for the Medal of Honor for heroism during service on the western front in World War I. He was awarded the Medal of Honor for his service in the Philippines during World War II. He was twice awarded the Distinguished Service Cross and seven times awarded the Silver Star.

MacArthur served as superintendent of the US Military Academy at West Point from 1919 to 1922. He instituted a number of reforms during his tenure at the Academy. He served as president of the United States Olympic Committee for the 1928 Amsterdam Summer Olympics. He was appointed chief of staff of the United States Army in 1930 and retired from the army in 1937, accepting a position as military advisor to the Commonwealth Government of the Philippines.

The Empire of Japan had been enlarging its military since the 1920s and had become a world power with expansionist ambitions. In 1931, Japan invaded Manchuria and established a client state in China, Manchukuo. In July 1937, Japan insisted on searching the Chinese city of Wanping for a missing soldier. China refused, so Japan attacked the city in a battle now known as the Marco Polo Bridge Incident. This led to a full-scale Japanese invasion, initiating the Second Sino-Japanese War (1937–45).

American war planners knew that the Empire of Japan had ambitions to conquer and annex the Philippines and other Asian lands. It was just a matter of time. General MacArthur, a beloved war hero in America, had the difficult assignment of preparing the Philippines for a seemingly inevitable invasion.

During a 1937 visit to Washington, DC, MacArthur urged the Navy Department to develop a new kind of vessel suited for the shallow inlets and islands of the Philippines. He called it a patrol torpedo boat, or PT boat—a small, fast boat armed with torpedoes and depth charges. The navy agreed with MacArthur and began developing PT boats for the Philippines. (A future American president, John F. Kennedy, would become a World War II hero as the skipper of PT-109.)

The Commonwealth of the Philippines was a protectorate of the United States and scheduled to achieve full independence in 1946. MacArthur accepted the task of organizing the armed forces of the Philippines so that the fledgling nation could defend itself. He restructured the Philippine Army, which consisted almost entirely of Filipinos plus a few American advisors. There was also a

US army garrison of about ten thousand soldiers, the Philippine Scouts, half of whom were Filipinos.

In July 1941, the army recalled sixty-one-year-old General MacArthur to serve as commander of the United States Armed Forces in the Far East. MacArthur merged the Philippine Army and the US Army's Philippine Scouts under a unified command.

Six months later, on December 7, 1941, Imperial Japan attacked the American naval base at Pearl Harbor, Hawaii. The following day, December 8, Japanese forces invaded the Philippines. The Japanese Navy blockaded the islands, making it impossible for the United States to evacuate its forces.

MacArthur, following the prewar plan he had drawn up in consultation with the United States War Department, declared the Philippine capital of Manila to be an open city—that is, Manila would offer no resistance to Japanese forces. In return, the invading forces were required under international law not to bomb or kill civilians as they moved in. This was to protect the people of Manila from the ravages of war. The Empire of Japan did not respect MacArthur's open city declaration and began bombing the city.

MacArthur moved his headquarters, along with the Philippine government, to the island fortress of Corregidor at the entrance to Manila Bay. The families of most US military and diplomatic personnel were flown out of the Philippines, but MacArthur's wife, Jean, and young son, Arthur MacArthur IV, remained with him on Corregidor (the boy was two months short of his fourth birthday). When someone asked MacArthur why he didn't send his son to safety in the States, he replied, "He is a soldier's son."

By March 1942, MacArthur's vastly outnumbered American and Philippine forces were forced to withdraw to the Bataan Peninsula on the west-central section of Luzon Island. There they made a heroic stand.

Back home, the American people had been hearing nothing but bad news ever since Pearl Harbor. Imperial Japan quickly conquered Burma, Malaya, Hong Kong, Singapore, the East Indies, and American bases on Guam and Wake Island. Tens of thousands of American and British troops were killed or taken prisoner. MacArthur's doomed but defiant stand in the Philippines inspired the American public despite the bad news from the front. MacArthur became the personification of Allied resistance to Imperial aggression.

General MacArthur sent a message to President Franklin D. Roosevelt stating that he and his family would remain on Corregidor and "share the fate of the garrison." But President Roosevelt, fearing that America's most famous and experienced general would be captured, ordered him to leave the Philippines and go to Australia.

The very thought of obeying that order, saving himself and leaving his troops behind, was abhorrent to MacArthur. He resented Roosevelt's order so much that he considered resigning his commission and becoming a volunteer in the Bataan defense force. His staff talked him out of it, saying that America was amassing such an overwhelming force in Australia that he would be able to return "almost at once . . . at the head of an effective rescue operation."[3] Had he known that he would not return to the Philippines for *two and a half years*, he might not have left at all.

Though deeply reluctant, MacArthur obeyed the order. He left Major General Jonathan M. Wainwright in command of American and Philippine forces on Corregidor and Bataan. "When I get back," MacArthur told Wainwright, "if you're still on Bataan, I'll make you a lieutenant general."

"I'll be on Bataan," Wainwright said, "if I'm still alive."[4]

It was an emotional moment for MacArthur. He had known Wainwright since West Point, when MacArthur was First Captain of the class of 1903 and Wainwright was a plebe.

(As it turned out, Wainwright survived the Bataan Death March and captivity as a prisoner of war. Soon after Wainwright was liberated in August 1945, MacArthur exceeded his promise, promoting him to a full four-star general. Wainwright was awarded the Medal of Honor and was privileged to witness the Japanese surrender aboard the battleship Missouri on September 2, 1945. He died in 1953.)

MacArthur told Major General George F. Moore, the Manila Harbor defense commander, "Keep the flag flying, George. I'm coming back."[5]

On the night of March 11, 1942, MacArthur, his family, and his senior staff (known as the Bataan Gang) boarded four PT boats, intending to break the Japanese blockade. MacArthur's foresight in calling for the creation of PT boats in 1937 probably saved his life and his family five years later.

Ahead of them lay a six-hundred-mile journey in PT boats, traveling mostly by night. The PT boats had already performed heroic service in the early months of the war and had to be mechanically overhauled before the trip. There were no replacement parts available, so some of the maintenance and repairs to the PT boats were of the Band-Aid-and-baling-wire variety. Each boat carried twenty fifty-five-gallon drums of fuel for the extended journey. Each passenger was allowed one piece of luggage, but MacArthur went empty-handed.

MacArthur was aboard PT-41, and the other boats in the formation were PTs 32, 34, and 35. If the boats encountered enemy ships, PT-41 was to escape while the others engaged the enemy. The boats got separated during the night, but late the next day three of the four boats converged at the rendezvous site, a cove on Tagauayan Island. One boat had to be abandoned, and the other two, PT-41 and PT-34, went on. At around sunset, the two boats saw a Japanese cruiser to the east, so they turned about and headed west toward the sun. The cruiser didn't pursue them and probably wasn't aware of them.

That night the weather and seas worsened. Twenty-foot waves crashed over the boat. Everyone aboard was soaked, cold, and seasick. The rough waters slowed their progress across the Mindanao Sea. They arrived at their next rendezvous point, Cagayan on Mindanao Island, at around sunup on March 13. After they pulled up to the wharf, MacArthur promised every member of the PT boat crew a Silver Star for gallantry. "You've taken me out of the jaws of death," he said, "and I won't forget it."[6]

A few hours after MacArthur arrived at Cagayan, the lost fourth boat, PT-35, pulled up at the wharf.

Meanwhile, Lieutenant General George H. Brett, commander of army forces in Australia, was trying to find a reliable airplane to bring MacArthur and his party from the Philippines to Australia. The only long-range aircraft he had in his inventory were some beat-up, shot-up Boeing B-17 Flying Fortresses that had seen a lot of action. He asked Vice Admiral Herbert Leary, commander of American naval forces in the Australia–New Zealand zone, to lend him a few of his brand-new navy B-17s for the MacArthur mission. Incredibly, Leary refused. (Sometimes interservice rivalry trumps the national interest.)

Brett had no choice but to send aging B-17s from an army bombardment group, even though they were practically death traps. Four planes took off, but two turned back because of engine trouble. A third plane crashed in the sea a few miles short of its destination, Del Monte Field on Mindanao (two crewmen were killed; the rest survived). One B-17 made it to Del Monte Field, but it had no brakes, and the supercharger, which enables the engine to run properly at high altitudes, had failed. The plane was completely unsuitable for such an important mission.

During MacArthur's second day on Mindanao, a Filipina woman showed up at Del Monte Plantation, where MacArthur was staying. She had walked twenty-five miles to talk to General MacArthur because her son was fighting in the north, and she hoped MacArthur could tell her if he was all right. Her visit surprised and alarmed MacArthur and his staff. If she knew that MacArthur was on Mindanao, then the Imperial Japanese might know as well. Japanese forces had already taken Davao City, a large port on the southern coast of Mindanao, just thirty miles away. For all they knew, the enemy might attack at any moment.

Back in Australia, General Brett called Admiral Leary again to repeat his request for navy B-17s. He expected another refusal. Instead, Leary was amazingly cordial and accommodating. Apparently, someone in Washington, DC, had adjusted his attitude. On March 16, two navy B-17s reached Del Monte Field by night, landing on a runway outlined by flares. After quickly refueling, the two bombers took off after midnight on March 17. General MacArthur rode in the radioman's seat. It was a cold, cramped flight to Australia.

Their intended destination was Darwin on the north-central coast of Australia. But as they approached Darwin, they learned the city was under attack. Darwin had already been devastated by a massive Japanese air raid on February 19, and the March 17 attack was one of more than a hundred follow-up raids to prevent Darwin from being used as an Allied base of operations. The two B-17s diverted to Batchelor Airfield, about fifty miles south of Darwin.

After his safe arrival in Australia, MacArthur told General Richard Sutherland, "It was close; but that's the way it is in war. You win or lose, live or die—and the difference is just an eyelash."[7] After refueling, the planes pushed on to Alice Springs, a thousand miles to the east, where MacArthur and his party could board a train for Melbourne.

The Australian government supplied a special train for General MacArthur and his family and staff. On March 20, the train pulled into Terowie Railway Station in south Australia. MacArthur's presence on the train was supposed to be a secret, but a crowd of Australian civilians was on hand, cheering as he stepped down from the train. He saluted his well-wishers, spotted a reporter, and told the reporter he had a statement to make that needed to reach the United States. The reporter assured him it would.

"The President of the United States," MacArthur said, "ordered me to break through the Japanese lines and proceed from Corregidor to Australia for the purpose, as I understand it, of organizing an American offensive against Japan, the primary purpose of which is the relief of the Philippines. I came through and I shall return."[8]

After making that statement, MacArthur rejoined his wife and son, and they boarded the train that would take them to Melbourne by way of Adelaide. On March 21, MacArthur's train pulled into Spencer Street Railway Station in Melbourne, and his journey ended. But the job of defeating the Empire of Japan was just beginning.

In Melbourne, MacArthur's staff from Corregidor, the Bataan Gang, helped him establish a new general headquarters. They remained at his side for the duration of the war. MacArthur had made a promise, "I shall return," and he kept it.

On October 20, 1944, two and a half years after leaving the Philippines, General MacArthur returned. He took a boat from the cruiser USS *Nashville* toward the shore of the island of Leyte. When the boat grounded in knee-deep water, MacArthur stepped out and waded ashore. Standing on Philippine territory, Mac-Arthur delivered a message to the Philippine nation:

> People of the Philippines: I have returned. By the grace of Almighty God our forces stand again on Philippine soil—soil consecrated in the blood of our two peoples. We have come dedicated and committed to the task of destroying every vestige of enemy control over your daily lives, and of restoring upon a foundation of indestructible strength, the liberties of your people.[9]

Pushing Japan's invasion forces out of the Philippines would take many more weeks of fighting. Finally, on March 2, 1945, Mac-Arthur returned to the island fortress of Corregidor. The general had a fondness for symbolism, so he and his staff, the Bataan Gang, returned to Corregidor the same way they had left—aboard four PT boats.

It is instructive to examine General Douglas MacArthur's choice of pronouns when he promised to return to the Philippines. He didn't say, "The army will be back," or "America will return," or (in some vague collective sense) "We will return." He said, definitively and quite personally, "I shall return."

He told General Wainwright, "When I get back, if you're still on Bataan, I'll make you a lieutenant general." He told General Moore, "Keep the flag flying, George. I'm coming back." He gave personal assurances, he gave his word, because he felt personally responsible for his troops, for his command, for the security of the Philippine Islands. His sense of personal responsibility was so deep and so strong that he could not walk away and say—as so many people today would say—"Well, I tried, but it's not my problem anymore."

He gave his personal pledge—"I shall return." And when he once again planted his feet on Philippine soil, he said, "I have returned."

During the two and a half years he was in Australia, directing the war effort in the Pacific theater and planning his return to the Philippines, MacArthur was deeply, intensely anguished to hear how his troops were faring under the Japanese occupation. The most bitter and painful experience of his career was receiving news of the Bataan Death March, in which seventy-six thousand prisoners of war—sixty-six thousand Filipinos and ten thousand Americans—were forced at the point of bayonets to march ninety miles down the Bataan Peninsula. At the end of that march, they were imprisoned at Camp O'Donnell, originally the base for the Philippine Army's Seventy-First Division but converted by Japanese occupation forces into a death camp. Soldiers died of thirst, sunstroke, disease, malnutrition, physical abuse, and wanton murder. At least three thousand Filipino and American soldiers died during the death march, and an additional twenty-seven to twenty-eight thousand are thought to have died at Camp O'Donnell.

When President Roosevelt ordered MacArthur to leave the Philippines, it was the most offensive order MacArthur had ever received. He came close to disobeying the order and even considered resigning his commission. He intended to keep his wife and four-year-old son on Corregidor and "share the fate of the garrison," so deep and intense was his sense of duty and responsibility.

I don't agree with MacArthur's decision to keep his wife and four-year-old son in the Philippines as the enemy was approaching. I respect MacArthur's sense of personal responsibility for himself, but I think he also had a responsibility to get his family out of harm's way. That being said, I think General MacArthur challenges us to take the virtue of responsibility seriously and to think about it deeply.

The West Point virtue of responsibility demands that we set high moral and ethical standards for ourselves and that we hold ourselves to those standards. When we fail to meet those standards, we have a responsibility to own up to our failure, accept the blame, and recommit ourselves to our high standards. We don't blame other people. We don't blame circumstances. We don't blame God. We accept full responsibility.

You may have had an unhappy childhood, abusive parents, tragedies, and injustices in your life. You are still responsible for your actions. Accept that responsibility. If you want to overcome the pain of the past, if you want to be successful and happy, then take full responsibility for your life. If you want to have good relationships, accept full responsibility for your relationships. If you want to have a successful career, accept full responsibility for your career. If you want to be healthy and fit, accept full responsibility for your exercise and diet and physical fitness.

Let's put an end to complaining. Let's put an end to blaming. Let's put an end to excuses. Let's accept full responsibility for our lives, our families, our communities, our nation, our world. Like Douglas MacArthur, West Point class of 1903, and Mike

Krzyzewski, West Point class of 1969, let's build the virtue of re-sponsibility into our lives. Let's be accountable to our God, to our better selves, and to one another.

Let's do our duty. Let's preserve our honor. Let's serve our country.

11

SERVICE

HUMBLE AND SELFLESS

In 1818, the United States Military Academy at West Point welcomed a distinguished visitor, Baron Alex Klinkowstrom, representing the Kingdom of Sweden. The baron served as a lieutenant colonel on Sweden's military staff and had come to study the American military training system.

During his tour, Baron Klinkowstrom visited a mathematics class and was surprised to see a Native American cadet at the blackboard, using trigonometry to determine the values of sine, cosine, and tangent for different angles. Baron Klinkowstrom watched the demonstration and spoke with the cadet after class. In his report to the Swedish government, he wrote, "This youth is a descendant of the Creek nation; his name is Moniac. In all probability he does not intend to go into the service of the United States, but to return to his people in order to give them the benefit of his achieved knowledge. He can also check the American surveyors in case the United States wishes to buy more land from the Creek territory."[1]

David Moniac, West Point class of 1822, was the first Native American to graduate from the Academy. He was born on Christmas Day 1802 at Pinchong Creek, Montgomery County, in what is now the state of Alabama. He was selected for admission to the Academy in 1817, when he was fifteen years old. At the time of his admission, Alabama was part of the Mississippi Territory; Alabama split from Mississippi in 1817 and was admitted to statehood in 1819, while Moniac was studying at West Point. So Moniac became the first Alabaman to attend West Point.

Some historians are baffled that Moniac, a Creek Indian, would attend West Point just three years after the end of the bitter and bloody Creek War of 1813–14, a war in which Moniac's own people suffered heavy losses and were defeated by the United States Army. The Upper Creeks, who went to war against the army, were led by Moniac's uncle, William Weatherford (also known as Chief Red Eagle). The Creek War ended with the Creek Nation being forced to surrender vast areas of land to the government. You would expect Moniac's allegiance to be to the Creeks, not the army. Yet Moniac chose to go to West Point. Why?

Part of the answer can be traced back to 1790, when Moniac's granduncle, Chief Alexander McGillivray (also known as Hoboi-Hili-Miko), the chief of the Upper Creek towns, negotiated a treaty with the federal government. One of the provisions of that treaty was that the United States would provide an education for four Creek young men. Moniac's father, Samuel Takkes-Hadjo Moniac, served as an interpreter during the negotiation of that treaty, which took place in New York City. After the treaty was signed, President George Washington personally presented a "peace medal" to Sam Moniac, and Sam treasured the medal, wore it every day, and was buried with it when he died.

From the time the treaty was signed in 1790 until the inauguration of President James Madison in 1809, David Moniac's father, Sam Moniac, spoke well of George Washington and the United States government, and he prospered as a rancher and a tavern keeper. But the government's relationship with the Indian nations changed after James Madison became president. The old promises were broken one by one. American settlers encroached on Indian land, often with help from the government. The Creeks were losing their culture and their way of life. Madison openly called for Native Americans to give up their traditions, to forsake hunting in favor of farming, and to become "civilized." So the Upper Creeks went to war against the American government (and the Americans' allies and trading partners, the Lower Creeks).

The Upper Creeks lost that war, and Sam Moniac lost everything he owned, including his farmland, herds, and tavern. But he was a practical man, and he knew that the only hope of getting anything back from the United States government was for his son, David, to take advantage of the education provision in the 1790 treaty. If David went to West Point, he not only would get a good education but also would be paid a monthly stipend as a cadet. So following the old principle of "If you can't beat 'em, join 'em," Sam encouraged David to go to West Point.

Before going to New York to begin training at West Point, David Moniac spent several weeks being tutored in Washington, DC, in preparation for the Academy entrance examination and curriculum. Throughout his time at West Point, Moniac would keep one foot in the world of West Point and the other in the world of the Creek traditions. As a boy, he became skilled at tracking and hunting deer. He knew how to survive in the wild and thrive amid the hardships of winter. He had listened to the wise teachings and proud oratory of his uncle, Chief William Weatherford, and his granduncle, Chief Alexander McGillivray.

Colonel Gilbert Christian Russell, an army officer who lived in Alabama and had fought in the Creek War, thought David

171

Moniac's appointment to West Point would help bring peace between the American government and the Creek Nation. On March 1, 1816, he wrote to Secretary of War William H. Crawford that David Moniac's father, Sam, was one of the "friendly Creeks" and that David would work hard and do well at West Point. "The distinguished McGillivray was the great uncle of the boy," Russell wrote. "His friends are numerous and powerful and are anxiously waiting the result of his application. Educated in our National Seminary [referring to West Point], he will acquire a permanent attachment to our Government and our laws."[2] In short, educating David Moniac at West Point was a matter of national self-interest.

Moniac began his studies at West Point at precisely the age when young Creek males go through initiation into manhood. In the Creek culture, manhood meant warriorhood. In some ways, Moniac's West Point training would serve as his initiation, his rite of passage into manhood. He was studious and respected the rules of the institution. The few demerits he earned were mostly the result of oversights, not misbehavior—oversleeping and missing roll call, failing to sign his stipend receipt, missing a military drill, talking in study hall. He got along well with his fellow cadets and was never disciplined for fighting or drinking.

He was not as academically gifted as some of his fellow cadets. He excelled in mathematics and tactics but struggled miserably in French (the French language was a core requirement because so many books on tactics and the military arts were written in that language during the Napoleonic era). He graduated thirty-ninth out of forty, but that is not as poor a showing as it sounds. There were 117 cadets in his class, and 79 didn't graduate. Thirty-ninth out of 117 cadets is not a bad showing at all.

Moniac's arrival at West Point coincided with the arrival of Sylvanus Thayer as superintendent of the Academy. His plebe year took place during a time of upheaval, as Thayer was attempting to institute academic and disciplinary reforms at West Point. Partly because of the chaos Thayer inherited from his predecessor, Alden Partridge, and partly because of Moniac's lack of early formal schooling, Moniac struggled through his first year at West Point. He decided to repeat his first year. As a result, it took him five years to graduate.

Thayer's reform effort triggered a crisis that Moniac helped to resolve. Superintendent Thayer had placed an army officer, Captain John Bliss, in command of the cadets. Thayer wanted a strict disciplinarian in that position, but Bliss was more than strict—he was physically abusive. During drills and marches, Bliss would pick up stones and hurl them at any cadet he felt was not executing the drill properly. On one occasion, he dragged one cadet out of the ranks by his collar, shook him roughly, and screamed at him.

One hundred eighty cadets signed a bill of particulars, accusing Bliss of being violent and abusive toward the cadets. Five cadets took the petition to Thayer's office, but the superintendent refused to speak to them or receive their petition. When the five cadets attempted to present the petition a second time, Thayer accused them of mutiny and ordered them to desist. The five cadets (Moniac was *not* one of them) walked off the base and gathered in a tavern to discuss their next move—so they were AWOL as well as mutineers.

Thayer dismissed the five cadets, then called for a court of inquiry to determine whether their dismissal should be upheld or reversed. During the inquiry, Moniac gave written testimony, on his honor, that "Captain John Bliss, without the least possible provocation, did throw stones at us, and at several other cadets of the Military Academy."[3] The court of inquiry found that the five dismissed cadets had in fact been mutinous and that Superintendent Thayer had acted properly by dismissing them. The court also found that Captain John Bliss was guilty of conduct unbecoming an officer and should be dismissed. There is no excuse for an officer to be violent and abusive, but the solution to an abusive officer is not mutiny. The decision of the court was upheld by Attorney General William Wirt.

Perhaps Moniac's experience with Creek tribal justice as the nephew of a chief had given him a perspective on one's duty toward authority figures that some of his fellow cadets lacked. Under tribal justice, there was no expectation that the chief's word would always be fair, but it always had to be respected and obeyed. Mutiny was not a solution in the Creek tribal system, and it wasn't a solution in the army. Moniac respectfully gave testimony when his testimony was required, but he would take no part in a mutinous action against authority.

In the Creek culture, the rite of passage into manhood included serving as a menial slave to the warriors, lighting their pipes, carrying their burdens, and brewing the ceremonial "black drink," a semipoisonous herb tea that induced excitement, intoxication, and sometimes vomiting as part of the initiation ritual. Moniac undoubtedly sensed a strong parallel between the rituals of West Point and the coming-of-age rituals of his own culture. He was at West Point to learn—and to serve.

Even though anti-Indian bias was common in the early 1800s, Moniac was accepted by his fellow cadets without prejudice. He made many friends and seemed to have no enemies, and perhaps that is because he was always eager to render service to others. During his final year at West Point, he befriended and mentored a fifteen-year-old first-year cadet, Maskell C. Ewing of Pennsylvania. Ewing, in a letter to his parents, mentioned that he had help in writing the letter from Cadet Moniac.

Life at West Point was challenging. The coursework was challenging. The discipline was challenging. Even the Academy accommodations were challenging. The West Point campus was isolated in those days and could be reached only by a riverboat on the Hudson River or by a rough and narrow dirt road that was impassable in the wintertime due to snow. Water for drinking or washing at the barracks had to be hauled from a well in buckets. Heat for the barracks in the wintertime was provided by wood stoves, and the wood had to be hauled by cadets from the wood yard. Barracks were sparsely furnished, and cadets bought many needed furnishings from the base store out of their monthly stipend.

But the lifestyle that many cadets considered a hardship seemed luxurious to Moniac. Hauling water and carrying firewood were not burdensome chores to him. Yes, the courses were challenging, and the intensive daily grind of classroom instruction and studying from books was totally new to him. But he was there to learn. And being isolated on the West Point campus was no problem for him—after all, where was he going to go?

In August 1821, the commandant of cadets, Major William Worth, a hero of the War of 1812 (and the man Fort Worth, Texas, is named for), marched two hundred cadets from West Point to Boston. There they performed a parade and precision drills for the aging former president John Adams. One of those two hundred cadets was David Moniac.

During their time in Boston, the cadets toured the battlefield at Bunker Hill and enjoyed a banquet in their honor on the Harvard University campus. They visited the home of John Adams in the neighboring village of Quincy. Adams—a founding father who helped Thomas Jefferson draft the Declaration of Independence—delivered a short speech to them on the value of their West Point education. After his speech, Adams wanted to meet the American Indian cadet, and Major Worth asked Cadet Moniac to step forward, but Moniac wouldn't move. Finally, Worth told the former president, "He is too bashful."

Was it mere bashfulness on Moniac's part? Or was it a more noble quality, such as humility? I think the evidence shows that Moniac was a young man with a serving heart and a sense of humility that came from his Creek culture. One of the great virtues of the Creek culture was that Creeks identified with their community. They did not seek individual attention or glory. Creek warriors were members of a band of warriors, and they did not seek to become individual heroes or celebrities.

Because of his culture, Moniac was uncomfortable being singled out for attention by President Adams. He identified as one cadet in the Corps of Cadets. He shunned the spotlight, as a good Creek warrior should. Even at West Point, he remained a Creek warrior to the bone. Ironically, his self-effacing Creek warrior ethos made him a better West Point cadet, because he remained focused on the West Point virtue of service and rejected any attempt to single him out as a special or notable individual.

❖❖❖

In April 1822, as David Moniac was nearing graduation, he opened a letter from an uncle who urged him to leave school and return home to Alabama as soon as possible. David's father, Sam, who had been a problem drinker for years, had become a full-blown drunk. While his mind was addled with alcohol, he had entered into a series of disastrous business deals and had dissipated much of the property belonging to his clan, the Creek Wind Clan. David's uncle urged him to immediately take charge of the family's financial duties before everything was gone.

David Moniac had only a little over two months to go to complete his degree and earn his army commission. He wasn't about to squander the investment he had made during the last five years of his life. He chose to stay and graduate with his class in June. Upon his graduation, he received a commission as a second lieutenant in the Sixth Infantry of the United States Army.

Then Moniac asked for and received a leave of absence, and he returned to Alabama, where he reorganized the family finances and established a plantation at Little River in Baldwin County. There he bred racehorses and raised cotton while looking after his father. He resigned from active duty in the army on December 31, 1822. He later married a Creek woman named Mary Powell, whose cousin Billy Powell was better known as Osceola, the Creek-born leader of the Seminoles in Florida.

For more than a dozen years, Moniac lived in peace with his wife in Alabama. They raised two children, a son and a daughter, and their farm prospered.

In 1836, a small band of displaced Creeks carried out raids in Alabama. The state of Alabama called up the militia, and Moniac reported for duty as an enlisted man, serving under General Thomas Sidney Jesup, the quartermaster general of the army and a veteran of the War of 1812. The uprising was quickly put down. A few months later, in October 1836, Moniac was called up again. The army commissioned him as a captain and placed him in charge of the all-Creek Regiment of Mounted Volunteers. The Second Seminole War had begun, and Captain Moniac was going to war in Florida.

In mid-November 1836, he led a successful charge against a Seminole fortification in an area where the city of Tampa stands today. For his courage and resourcefulness, Moniac received a brevet promotion to major.

About a week later, on November 21, the Regiment of Mounted Volunteers, the Florida Militia (under the command of Brigadier General Richard K. Call), and a number of Tennessee Volunteers gathered at the edge of Wahoo Swamp (about seventy miles north of modern-day Tampa). Some twenty-five hundred soldiers formed a mile-long line. Major Moniac commanded about six hundred Creek and Choctaw soldiers. Ironically, one of Moniac's objectives was to kill or capture Osceola, his wife's cousin, the leader of the Seminoles.

As they moved into the open space of the swamp, the Seminoles war whooped and fired at them from behind trees. The troops returned fire and moved forward. The gun battle was fierce and bloody on both sides, and the terrain grew muddier as the troops advanced. Some of the government troops advanced quickly, others straggled, and the line became disorganized. The Seminoles fell back, crossed a muddy stream, regrouped, and began firing at the troops. The Seminole fusillade was so intense that it stopped the soldiers' advance.

Moniac rallied his troops and charged into the stream with his men following close behind. He waded into the water, and the Seminoles opened fire on him, hitting him multiple times. He tumbled face-first into the water and sank from sight.

The Seminoles, thinking they had felled the chief of the Creeks, came out of hiding, whooping and celebrating. The troops moved up to the river's edge, firing repeatedly, and forced the Seminoles to retreat. Some of the men wanted to ford the river and pursue the Seminoles, but General Call ordered his troops to withdraw because it was late in the day. Major Moniac's men retrieved his body from the stream, and the Battle of Wahoo Swamp ended inconclusively.

General Jesup later eulogized David Moniac, saying he was as brave and gallant a man as ever drew a sword or faced an enemy.

Selfless service is one of the seven Army values. The other six are loyalty, duty, respect, honor, integrity, and personal courage. The army defines selfless service in this statement: "Put the welfare of the Nation, the Army and your subordinates before your own."[4]

To practice the West Point virtue of service, you have to recognize, first, that you are part of something much bigger than yourself. Many, perhaps most, people in the world live to serve themselves. But in the army, you learn to put the welfare of your country, the army, and your subordinates before your own welfare. You serve without expecting any recognition or personal gain. West Point seeks to instill in its cadets not just a code of ethics but the spirit of a warrior culture, which it calls "the warrior ethos."

> I will always place the mission first.
> I will never accept defeat.
> I will never quit.
> I will never leave a fallen comrade.[5]

Was David Moniac ever conflicted? Did he ever wonder where his duty lay? Did he ever wonder whether he owed honor and allegiance to the Creek Nation or to the United States of America? If he was conflicted, he didn't show it. He always seemed to maintain his allegiance to America and American ideals, to West Point and its traditions and its discipline, and to the army and its values.

Perhaps his values were shaped by his father, Sam, who never forgot the day President George Washington gave him a medal and told him that it stood for peace between the Creek people and the people of the United States. Later, when President Madison altered the government's relationship with Native Americans and called on the tribes to forsake their traditions and culture, David Moniac may have realized that the American government doesn't always obey its own founding principles.

At West Point, Moniac was steeped in the history and traditions of America and the rich meaning of America's founding documents, the Declaration of Independence and the Constitution of the United States. From the declaration, Moniac learned that the American spirit is expressed in these words: "We hold these truths to be self-evident, that all men are created equal, that they are endowed by their Creator with certain unalienable Rights, that among these are Life, Liberty and the pursuit of Happiness."

Those are inspiring words, even though our government was not living up to them at the time and has violated them many times throughout the years. The government betrayed those words when it pushed Native Americans off their land and when it permitted the enslavement of people who were brought here from Africa. Even the man who wrote those words, Thomas Jefferson, wasn't living up to them when he wrote them, because he was a slaveholder. But that doesn't make the words of the Declaration of Independence any less true or any less inspiring.

Perhaps Moniac was inspired by those words; inspired by the West Point ethos of duty, honor, and country; inspired by the army's tradition of selfless service. And perhaps he was also inspired by the warrior ethos of the Creek culture, the values taught to him by his uncle and granduncle, who were chiefs among the Creeks.

It is impossible to know all the influences that shaped Moniac's life and his commitment to service. We just know he was dedicated to living out the West Point virtues during his five years of training there. We know he was committed to serving and mentoring at least one young cadet and probably many others. We know he had the self-effacing humility of a warrior who is committed to selfless service. We know he was willing to answer the call of his family and serve the needs of his clan. We know he was willing to answer the call of his country, even to the point of sacrificing his life.

We don't know if Moniac ever heard the phrase "selfless service." We just know he lived it. A US soldier serves the nation, the people, and the Constitution and places full trust in America's free, democratic system of government. Those who have been in combat have an appreciation for the price of freedom that the people they protect can't fully understand. Those who have worn the uniform have a deeper understanding of what the phrase "selfless service" truly means.

That word *serve* is tossed around far too casually these days. We need to remember what it really means when we say that a soldier *serves* in the military. Whether man or woman, enlisted or commissioned officer, a soldier serves in ways that few civilians fully appreciate. Throughout our nation's history, generations of Americans have enjoyed freedom and prosperity because American soldiers have selflessly served their country. Soldiers don't make the policies or declare the wars. They simply serve, fight, and all too often die. They do so willingly and sacrificially, and their families often pay as high a price as they do.

Even if you are a civilian, you can selflessly serve your country. You can volunteer your time and tutor kids in an after-school program, coach youth sports, be a youth leader or Sunday school teacher in your church, visit lonely people in the nursing home, or befriend and serve an elderly neighbor. Join the Peace Corps or do short-term missionary work through your church. Start a business and create some jobs. Become a teacher or coach. Build homes for the poor through Habitat for Humanity. Adopt or foster a child. Give generously to the Salvation Army, Prison Fellowship, World Vision, or other worthy charities. Find a need that moves you and motivates you, then give of yourself to serve others and your country.

You can do your part to keep America free, strong, and welcoming to returning soldiers. Thank soldiers for their service and give them a smile and a handshake. Listen to soldiers, ask them questions, and offer to buy them a meal. Support veterans and organizations that serve veterans, such as Fisher House, Semper Fi Fund, Disabled American Veterans, Hope for the Warriors, and Hire Heroes USA. There is nothing wrong with "bumper sticker support" or "hashtag support" for veterans, but if you really want to thank a veteran in a meaningful way, find ways to selflessly serve veterans and their families.

Whether as civilians or as soldiers, we can all do selfless acts of service—for duty, honor, and country.

12

TRUST

THE GI'S GENERAL

Gneral of the Army Omar Bradley, West Point class of 1915, was born in a log cabin in Randolph County, Missouri, on February 12, 1893. From humble beginnings, he rose to become general of the army. He served with distinction during World War II and the Korean War.

As a boy, Omar Bradley would walk to school with his father, John Smith Bradley, and they would talk about faith, books, baseball, what it means to be a man, and the importance of a good education. Omar's father was a schoolteacher who walked several miles from his farm to a one-room schoolhouse in Higbee, where Omar was one of his star pupils. John Bradley invested a great deal of time mentoring Omar and laying a foundation of honesty, responsibility, and humility in his life. Father and son would read and discuss books together, go hunting and fishing together, and play catch to sharpen Omar's baseball skills. Young Omar Bradley enjoyed the time he spent talking to his father and learning from him.

Daily chores were a big part of young Omar's life. He gathered wood for the stove and fetched water from the well. His father had beehives and sold honey, and Omar helped his dad collect the honey from the hives, often at the expense of several stings. Omar hunted rabbits, skinned them, and sold the pelts, using the proceeds to buy ammunition for more rabbit hunting.

Every Sunday Omar put on his best suit and walked to church with his father, John, and his mother, Elizabeth (or Bessie, as she was called). They attended the Central Christian Church, a huge, high-steepled stone edifice with a large congregation.

In 1908, when Omar was nearing his fifteenth birthday, John Bradley died of pneumonia at age forty-one. It was a devastating blow to young Omar. He had always counted on his father's wisdom, encouragement, and support. After the funeral, Omar's mother decided they should move to the nearby town of Moberly. There she worked as a seamstress, while Omar delivered newspapers to supplement the family income.

Omar graduated from Moberly High School in 1910 and took a job as a clerk and boiler repairman with the Wabash Railroad, making seventeen cents an hour. His goal was to save enough money in one year to attend the University of Missouri in Columbia. There he planned to pursue a law degree.

One Sunday night in the spring of 1911, John Crewson, the Sunday school superintendent at Central Christian Church, took Omar aside and said, "Have you ever thought of applying for an appointment to West Point?" Crewson had become a friend and mentor to Omar following the death of his father.

"I could never afford to go to West Point," Omar said. "I'll have a hard enough time working my way through the University of Missouri."

"You don't pay to go to West Point," Crewson said. "If you get an appointment to the Academy, the army will pay you every month." At Crewson's suggestion, Omar wrote to his congressman, William W. Rucker of the Second District of Missouri, and asked for an appointment. The congressman wrote back and said that a candidate named Dempsey Anderson had already been selected, but Omar could take the entrance exam and possibly qualify as an alternate.

Omar had less than a week to study for the exam, to be offered in St. Louis, 150 miles away. Could he afford to take time off work and purchase a railroad ticket to St. Louis when he had so little chance of passing the test? Omar talked to a friend of his father's, a man who had advised him several times after his father passed away. The man said, "Go ahead and give it a try, Omar. Talk to your boss at the railroad. Since you're an employee, maybe they'll give you a pass to make the trip."

Omar decided that if he could get a free railroad pass, he would go to St. Louis. As it turned out, his boss at the Wabash Railroad was happy to encourage his West Point aspirations. Railroad pass in hand, Omar went to St. Louis.

The exam covered a range of subjects, from English to geography to math, and was conducted over a four-day period. Though Omar had excelled in algebra in high school, he hadn't used any algebraic knowledge during the year he had worked for the Wabash Railroad. His mind froze under the pressure. The formulas and theorems wouldn't come to him. Despairing, he got up and took his nearly blank test paper to the proctor, but the proctor was reading a book and ignored him.

Not wanting to annoy the proctor, Omar took the paper back to his desk—and the answers started coming to him. He ended up with a passing score on the algebra section and the top score on the total exam among Missouri applicants.

A few weeks after the exam, Omar Bradley opened a telegram that congratulated him and ordered him to report to the United

States Military Academy at West Point before noon on August 1, 1911. Omar thought it was a mistake. He phoned the other candidate, Dempsey Anderson, certain he had gotten the telegram intended for Dempsey. But Dempsey said he had failed to score high enough on the exam. Omar offered to decline the appointment so that Dempsey could go. Dempsey said, "Indeed not. You have won."[1]

Early in his life, Omar Bradley exhibited character traits that would mark his career as a leader—traits of selflessness, humility, sensitivity to the feelings of others, and an eagerness to see that others are treated fairly. It is because of these and other traits in Bradley's life that he came to be known as "the GI's General."

—◆—

Omar Bradley was a member of the West Point class of 1915, "the class the stars fell on." Of the 164 graduates of the class of 1915, fifty-nine (more than a third) achieved the rank of general—more than from any other class in the history of the Academy. Two members of the class attained a five-star rank—Dwight D. Eisenhower (who went on to become president of the United States) and Omar Bradley (who became chairman of the Joint Chiefs of Staff).

Eisenhower was one of Bradley's best friends at West Point. Both were members of Company F, and both played on the West Point football team. Eisenhower was the editor of *Howitzer*, the West Point yearbook, during their final year, and he wrote a character description of Bradley for the yearbook: "His most prominent characteristic is 'getting there,' and if he keeps up the clip he's started, some of us will some day be bragging to our grandchildren that 'sure, General Bradley was a classmate of mine.'"[2]

Though he was known throughout his life for his soft-spoken demeanor and compassion, Bradley was no pushover. On the football field, Bradley was a fierce competitor, even in practice scrimmages. In one practice, Cadet James Van Fleet (who later became a four-star general) was the running back. He was carrying the ball through a gap in the offensive line—until he was stopped cold by defensive lineman Bradley. For the rest of his life, Van Fleet had a scar along his left jaw, a reminder of how hard Bradley hit the line.

Life at West Point was largely governed by two concepts: West Point tradition and the West Point honor code. When Bradley was at West Point, the honor code was unwritten but clearly understood: "A cadet will not lie, cheat, or steal." Years later, the honor code was formalized and amended to read, "A cadet will not lie, cheat, or steal, or tolerate those who do." The West Point honor code was such a powerful force in shaping the character of cadets that, as Eisenhower once observed, it "seems to grow in importance with the graduate as the years recede until it becomes something that he is almost reluctant to talk about—it occupies in his mind a position akin to the virtue of his mother or his sister."[3] Few other institutions of higher learning exert such an influence over the rest of their graduates' lives.

The strict West Point code of conduct could be challenging for some cadets, but Bradley didn't find it difficult to live up to. It was merely an extension of the code his father had instilled in him. In fact, West Point's rigorous code of conduct, with its focus on duty and honor, strongly appealed to him.

Bradley graduated forty-fourth out of a class of 164. For almost three decades after graduation, Bradley had relatively little contact with his friend Dwight Eisenhower. They saw each other at the occasional reunion or Army-Navy game but didn't serve together at the same army base or outpost.

Soon after graduation in 1915, Bradley was posted with the Fourteenth Infantry Regiment in Spokane, Washington. An enlisted man on the base was accused of theft and learned that Second Lieutenant Bradley had studied military law at West Point. The man asked Bradley to represent him at his court-martial. It seemed to be an open-and-shut case against the soldier, but

Bradley won an acquittal. After that, every prisoner in the stockade wanted Bradley to represent him at trial. He took on a number of cases, winning most of them.

Finally, the base commander got tired of watching miscreants beat the rap, so he appointed Bradley to serve as a member of the court. Once Bradley switched from defense counsel to prosecution, defendants began losing almost every time—and the base commander was happy.

An incident that took place in Spokane on New Year's Eve 1915 gave an indication of the kind of leader and problem solver Bradley would one day become. He was walking along the street that night when he saw a group of drunk civilians brawling with a group of drunk soldiers from the base. Risking life and limb, Bradley positioned himself between the two groups and began talking to the soldiers as if he were their football coach instead of a wet-behind-the-ears second lieutenant fresh out of West Point. "Come on, men, let's get along home," he shouted to them.

He spoke with a tone that was part military authority and part friendly persuasion. He didn't have to threaten. He didn't have to hit anybody. No one got arrested. The fight simply broke up, and everyone went their separate ways. That result was typical of Bradley's easygoing style of conflict resolution.

During World War I, many of Bradley's West Point comrades went to France with the American Expeditionary Force. Bradley's infantry regiment, however, was sent to Montana to guard copper mines during a strike. Bradley was miserable and feared that being kept out of combat duty would ruin his career.

In 1920, Bradley returned to West Point to teach mathematics. Four years later, he went to Georgia to study at the Infantry School at Fort Benning. He finished second in his class.

After infantry school, he was assigned to the Twenty-Seventh Infantry Regiment in Hawaii, where he had plenty of time to improve his golf game (he got his handicap down to four). While in Hawaii, he met George S. Patton. One time Patton invited Bradley to go trapshooting, using clay pigeons. Bradley missed his first two shots, then hit twenty-three in a row. Patton smiled and said, "You'll do."

Bradley spent three years in Hawaii, and though he loved the weather and the people, he found the duty boring. He leaped at the chance to spend a year studying at the Command and General Staff College at Fort Leavenworth, Kansas. When George C. Marshall offered him an opportunity to become an instructor at the Infantry School at Fort Benning, he was ready. His stint at Fort Benning would prove to be one of the most important breaks in his career, and George Marshall would become one of the most influential people in his life.

As colleagues and soldiers, Bradley and Marshall worked well together. Both were serious about making sure America was ready to fight its next war. Both disapproved of vices such as smoking and telling dirty jokes. Both were outdoorsmen who liked to hunt. And both respected talent and good character in others.

Marshall named Bradley to head the weapons section of the Infantry School at Fort Benning. In his final fitness report on Bradley, Marshall wrote, "Quiet, unassuming, capable, sound common sense. Absolute dependability. Give him a job and forget it. Recommended command: Regiment in peace, division in war."[4]

Because of Marshall, Bradley learned to become a confident public speaker. Marshall would not permit his instructors to deliver their lectures from notes. Every instructor had to learn to speak extemporaneously. Though Bradley initially tried to leave note cards on the floor where they couldn't be seen, he eventually developed the skill and confidence of speaking without notes. The speaker who can simply have a conversation with an audience builds trust with the listeners.

Bradley also learned a key leadership principle from Marshall: delegate authority to your subordinates, empower them to make decisions, and let them do their job. Bradley observed, "Once having assigned an officer to his job, General Marshall seldom intervened."[5] Bradley emulated Marshall's delegating style, and it served him well throughout his career.

One surprising feature of Marshall's approach to leadership was that he allowed his aides to challenge his ideas. Marshall wanted to have the widest range of options to choose from, the widest span of opinions to inform his judgment. At the end of Bradley's first week at the Infantry School, Marshall gave him a major chewing out. Why? During the whole week, Bradley hadn't disagreed with Marshall even once.

Bradley learned many such leadership lessons from Marshall at Fort Benning. He took many of those lessons with him into World War II.

In 1939, Marshall was selected as army chief of staff, and he appointed Bradley to serve on his general staff. Bradley worked at the old Munitions Building on Constitution Avenue in Washington, DC. His chief job was to present decision papers to Chief of Staff Marshall. In 1941, Marshall promoted Bradley and appointed him commandant of the Infantry School at Fort Benning.

One Sunday afternoon in December, Bradley and his wife, Mary, were in the front yard of their Fort Benning home when a car screeched to a stop in the street beyond their front gate. A fellow Fort Benning instructor, Harold Bull, shouted to the Bradleys from the car, "Did you hear about Pearl Harbor?"

That day, December 7, 1941, Bradley's life changed forever. His time of testing was about to begin.

◆◈◆◈◆

Promoted to the rank of major general, Bradley took command of the Eighty-Second Division; later, he took command of the Twenty-Eighth (National Guard) Division. He found both units underequipped, undertrained, and ill-prepared for war. Soldiers were using broomsticks as stand-ins for rifles. Bradley quickly earned a reputation as a leader who could take a disorganized, demoralized division and transform it into a highly motivated fighting force.

In February 1943, Bradley joined his old West Point friend, Dwight Eisenhower, at Ike's headquarters in Tunisia. Born in 1893, Bradley was fifty years old and had never been in combat. He had proven himself to be an organizational genius who knew how to motivate soldiers and lift their morale. He had proven himself to be a great teacher of tactics and military history. His wisdom was respected by many battle-hardened veterans of war—but his leadership had never been tested on the battlefield.

Days earlier, American forces under General Lloyd Fredendall had suffered a humiliating, costly defeat at Kasserine Pass in Tunisia. The German Tenth Panzer Division under Field Marshal Erwin Rommel was advancing like a juggernaut. Eisenhower showed Bradley a map of the American retreat and said he wanted ideas for turning the situation around—*fast*. Bradley told Eisenhower he would investigate, then offer his recommendations.

Long before management consultants Tom Peters and Robert H. Waterman used the term "management by walking around" in their 1982 book *In Search of Excellence*, Bradley practiced this management style at II Corps in Tunisia. He went around to various combat units and told them he was looking for ideas to improve combat training in the States. Well, it was a little white lie—and it got him what he wanted.

Officers, noncommissioned officers, and enlisted men laid it on the line. They told Bradley what was wrong with leadership, what was wrong with the strategy, and what was wrong with the equipment they had been given (from rifles that jammed to tanks and half-tracks that were too lightly armored). By talking to the soldiers who were doing the fighting, Bradley learned that leadership was disorganized, the Corps lacked discipline, and morale was nonexistent.

After Bradley made his report, Eisenhower relieved General Fredendall and placed II Corps under the command of George S. Patton Jr. At Patton's insistence, Bradley was named deputy commander of II Corps. Later, after Patton took command of the

Seventh Army in preparation for the invasion of Sicily, Bradley took command of II Corps. Bradley ably led II Corps in the closing days of the Tunisia campaign and throughout the Sicily campaign of July and August 1943.

<hr />

Field Marshal Bernard "Monty" Montgomery, commander of the British Eighth Army, was a master of self-promotion. He had a press office in his camp to manage relations with reporters. So did General George S. Patton. Omar Bradley could not have cared less about his public image or what the newspaper reporters were writing about him. It wasn't that he was shy. He was simply indifferent to public perception. His father had raised him to see bragging and self-promotion as unseemly. Such deeply ingrained humility was rare among those who wore the stars of an army general.

In August 1943, during the Sicily campaign, famed war correspondent Ernie Pyle contacted Bradley's staff, seeking permission to travel with General Bradley so that he could write about the war effort from a commander's perspective. This was an unusual angle for Pyle, whose enormously popular newspaper columns were usually written from the point of view of the combat GI, the average soldier, not the generals. Since the war had begun, he had not profiled a general until he approached Bradley. But Eisenhower had given Ernie Pyle a piece of advice: "Go discover Bradley."

When the publicity-shy Bradley heard that Pyle wanted to talk to him, he wasn't interested. He had a war to fight and eighty thousand soldiers to take care of. He flatly rejected Pyle's request—at first.

But General Bradley's aide, Chet Hansen, countered that Americans wanted to know who was leading the troops. American women wanted to know who was taking care of their husbands and sons on the battlefield. Bradley would raise morale back home and on the battlefield, Hansen said, if he would give Pyle the access he wanted.

The morale argument made sense to Bradley, and he agreed to allow Pyle to travel with him for three days.

So Pyle tagged along with Bradley, ate meals with him, interviewed him, and even survived a German dive bomber attack with him. Bradley was wary of the newsman at first but eventually opened up. They had deep talks about the responsibility and the morality of having to kill people in war. Bradley admitted that some of the orders he gave—whether bombing an enemy city or sending his own troops into harm's way—often troubled his sleep. But he was reconciled to his duty, and he did it all without hesitation to protect civilization from the barbarism of the Nazis.

Pyle also talked to soldiers who had stories to tell about General Bradley, and they were all stories about Bradley's kindness and generosity, stories about the general asking the troops about their families back home, stories about Bradley giving soldiers cigarettes, stories about Bradley lending money to his troops and never asking for repayment. Pyle wrote a six-part newspaper feature in which he dubbed Bradley "the GI's General." The label stuck. As Pyle explained, "I am a tremendous admirer of General Bradley. I don't believe I have ever known a person to be so unanimously loved and respected by the men around him."[6]

After the successful completion of the Sicily campaign, Eisenhower placed Bradley in command of the US First Army. He also made Bradley a top planner for the D-Day invasion of Normandy. Bradley also devised a plan called Operation Cobra, which was implemented on July 25, 1944, designed to send Bradley's First Army and Patton's Third Army rolling into Brittany, collapsing the German defenses and reversing the course of World War II. According to historian Jim DeFelice, "Bradley, even more than Eisenhower" was "the architect of the American victory in Europe."[7]

From D-Day until the end of the war in Europe, Bradley would command more forces than any other general in US history: four armies, twelve corps, forty-eight divisions—a total of 1.3 million soldiers.

A few days before the Allied invasion of Normandy on D-Day, June 6, 1944, General Bradley gathered his corps and division commanders in Bristol for a review of the invasion plan. Bradley— the Missouri schoolteacher's son, the longtime instructor at West Point and the Infantry School at Fort Benning—stood at the front of the room with a pointer in his hand and a large map of France behind him. His "students" all had stars on their collars. They were the army generals whose troops would carry out the largest military operation in human history. Bradley called each one to the front of the room. One by one, they came up, pointed to the map, and described what their units would do on that fateful morning.

Each general knew his assignment and how his outfit's actions fit into the overall plan of battle. They were ready to begin the liberation of Europe.

Once each general had spoken, it was Bradley's turn. He clasped his hands behind him. His eyes glistened with emotion. Then he said, simply and sincerely, "Good luck, men."

<hr />

During the final weeks before D-Day, General Bradley spent as much time as he could with the troops. He toured the bases around southern England, where American troops were preparing for the ordeal ahead. He watched them conduct mortar practice, rifle practice, bayonet exercises, and timed obstacle courses. Once they hit the beaches, those men would need to react reflexively, instinctively to the dangers they faced. Nothing could really prepare anyone for what the German war machine would throw at them, but those soldiers were as physically and mentally conditioned as was humanly possible.

After watching the brave GIs go through their paces, he would always give them a brief word of encouragement, concluding with a jaunty, "I will see you on the beaches!"

Just four years earlier, Bradley had been a lieutenant colonel, an aide to General Marshall, taking the bus to the old Munitions Building on Constitution Avenue in Washington, DC. And just sixteen months earlier, he had arrived in Tunisia as a "book general" without any combat experience—a man who seemed more like a schoolteacher than a warrior. Yet as of June 1944, he was the senior commander of American ground forces for the invasion code-named Operation Overlord. In that capacity, Bradley was the architect of the ultimate defeat of Hitler's Third Reich.

The Normandy invasion on Tuesday, June 6, 1944, was the largest seaborne invasion in history. Nothing like it had ever been attempted before, and nothing like it has been attempted since. Nearly 5,000 landing and assault craft, 289 escort ships, and 277 minesweepers took part in the operation. Some 160,000 troops hit the beaches that day, and 875,000 troops had disembarked by the end of June. The Allies suffered 10,000 casualties the first day, including 4,414 confirmed dead. General Bradley came ashore less than twenty-four hours after the invasion began.

Commanding the First Army, and ultimately the Twelfth Army Group, General Bradley led his soldiers across France and into Germany, until he joined up with Marshal Ivan Stepanovich Konev, commander of the Soviet Red Army, at the Elbe River on April 25, 1945. At that historic moment, Nazi Germany was finished as a military power. General Omar Bradley had proven he was not only a brilliant tactician in the classroom but also a brilliant leader on the battlefield.

When General Bradley visited Marshal Konev at the Soviet field headquarters, Konev provided entertainment in the form of a troupe of Russian ballerinas, performing gracefully to music played on a Victrola. It was a strange sight to witness after experiencing months of death, destruction, and all-out war. After the performance, Konev informed General Bradley that the graceful female dancers were all gun-toting soldiers in the Red Army.

Bradley then invited Marshal Konev to enjoy his hospitality at the American field headquarters. It was Marshal Konev's turn to be surprised. Bradley introduced him to the Russian-American violinist Jascha Heifetz, who had traveled across Europe with the Allied troops, performing on the piano and violin, both classical and jazz compositions, in the mess halls of army camps.

After Germany capitulated, Bradley returned to a hero's welcome in the United States. He had taken care of his troops as a general in wartime. Postwar, he became head of the Veterans Administration from 1945 to 1947, and he took care of the troops in peacetime. Later, he served as chief of staff of the army and then as chairman of the Joint Chiefs of Staff. In 1950, he was promoted to the rank of five-star general. He was one of four men in American history to hold the title General of the Army (the other three: Henry H. "Hap" Arnold, Douglas MacArthur, and George C. Marshall; another five-star general, John J. Pershing, held the title General of the Armies).

Omar Bradley never retired. A general of the army holds that title for life and may be recalled to active duty whenever his nation needs him. In 1969, following the death of former president Dwight D. Eisenhower, Omar Bradley became the last living five-star general. He attended the inauguration of President Ronald Reagan in January 1981 and died of a heart attack on April 8 of that year in New York City. He was eighty-eight years old.

Omar Bradley was a little over six feet tall with a lean, athletic build. He wore round-lensed, wire-rimmed spectacles. He always stood with straight military rectitude, yet he was one of the most casually dressed generals on any battlefield. He was often found wearing standard GI trousers tucked into paratroop boots, with an infantry field cap on his head. In cold weather, he wore a trench coat that had seen better days. Journalist A. J. Liebling of the *New Yorker* once called him "the least dressed-up commander of an American army in the field since Zachary Taylor, who wore a straw hat."[8] His demeanor was always genial, unpretentious, and soft-spoken. Eisenhower hailed him as "the master tactician of our forces" and "America's foremost battle leader."[9] Yet Bradley's troops found him approachable, humble, and easy to talk to. He was a man of great character, a leader of great competence, and a general who loved and cared for his soldiers. The Austrian psychologist Alfred Adler once said, "Men of genius are admired, men of wealth are envied, men of power are feared; but only men of character are trusted."[10] Bradley was a man of character. He earned the trust of the soldiers he led.

Because his soldiers trusted him, they readily followed him onto the beaches of Normandy, across the fields of France, into the dark abyss of Nazi Germany, and all the way to the banks of the Elbe River. They followed him because they knew he cared about them, he wouldn't needlessly waste their lives, and he would lead them to victory.

One of Bradley's biographers, Jim DeFelice, described the quiet, sturdy character of Bradley and explained how he earned the trust of his troops and how he used that trust to achieve victory on the battlefield:

> Bradley was a man of moderate behavior, a mature leader who thought before he spoke, who risked his life but didn't call attention to it. He allowed his subordinates to take credit and glory. When he disagreed with his superiors, he did so discreetly. He dressed for the field, and looked it. He lived, for much of the war, in a truck. . . .
>
> Bradley was, first and last, a believer in values that, even during the War, would have been cynically termed "small-town"—self-reliance, respect for others, humility. He was the product of an America that had only recently conquered the frontier, an America where brain and brawn fit together naturally . . . an America where calling attention to one's achievements cheapened them irrevocably.

When so much of our perception of history depends on drama and flash, is there room for a man who personified quiet competence? *Yes.* For beyond the flash and drama of the moment, the real achievements of the war depended on men like Bradley. And still do.[11]

General Bradley would be the first to tell you that battles are not won by generals. Battles are won by the soldiers on the battlefield. Generals design the strategy, but soldiers fight the battle. To fight with confidence and a strong morale, a soldier must have trust in the leader who designed the strategy. General Bradley once said that for soldiers to trust a leader, the leader must have good character. He explained what character meant to him and why character engendered trust in a leader:

> Dependability, integrity, the characteristic of never knowingly doing anything wrong, that you would never cheat anyone, that you would give everybody a fair deal. Character is a sort of an all-inclusive thing. If a man has character, everyone has confidence in him. Soldiers must have confidence in their leader.[12]

After his retirement, Bradley gave a speech in which he described what he considered to be the most important qualities a leader must have: strong character, perseverance, mental acuity, physical energy—and one more thing, a quality he called "human understanding." He cited Abraham Lincoln as the greatest role model of this quality:

> Lincoln, to my mind, had this in greater measure than any other man in history—the ability to understand the problems of those who served under him, and to appreciate their feelings in every situation. This includes, in my opinion, regular words of praise, as well as the occasional obligation for words of constructive criticism. It includes a great appreciation for an individual's privacy: Criticism of a man should be given personally, not through impersonal communication, and in privacy, not in public. . . . Most of all, human

198

understanding is exemplified when a superior listens—and listens attentively—when his subordinates are asked to give their opinions, or when they voluntarily come forward with an idea.[13]

Bradley became a general of the army because of his tactical brilliance. But he became the GI's General because he earned the trust of his soldiers.

✦◆◆✦

The West Point virtue of trust is essential to leadership—and it is essential to winning the battles of our lives, whether on the battlefield, on the sports field, in the medical field, in the field of ministry, or in the field of business and commerce. Trust is the glue that holds a team, organization, church, or military unit together. When we trust one another, we can accomplish great things. Without trust, we are defeated before we begin.

Trust turns a loose collection of individuals into a tightly unified team. When we trust each other, we care for each other. When we care for each other, we can motivate and energize each other to accomplish anything.

How did General Omar Bradley build trust with his troops? He built trust with a combination of character and caring. A leader of character tells the truth, and truth is the foundation of trust. And Bradley's troops knew he cared about them. He visited them, talked to them, leveled with them, and listened to them.

Bradley's father taught him the importance of traits such as honesty, responsibility, hard work, humility, and faith in God. When people saw these traits in Bradley's life, they naturally wanted to trust him and follow him as a leader. In his youth, he was the kind of man who would willingly sacrifice his own admission to West Point out of a sense of fairness to the other guy. In his later years, Bradley took the helm of the Veterans Administration and tackled the job of making the VA bureaucracy responsive to the needs of America's returning warriors.

Bradley, just months after his graduation from West Point, demonstrated authority, tempered with friendly persuasion. He managed to get a bunch of brawling drunks on New Year's Eve to go their separate ways without further violence or arrests. Bradley's remarkable ability to defuse potentially explosive situations is a rare and valuable leadership skill.

One often-overlooked means of gaining trust, especially as a leader, is the ability to deliver a speech without notes. From George Marshall, Bradley learned how to speak extemporaneously. Leaders who can give a presentation in a relaxed and conversational way are more persuasive than boring speakers who read their notes or anxious speakers who make people uneasy. When you have a conversation with your audience, they relax and trust you.

Bradley also learned from Marshall how to lead by delegating, how to let people make their own decisions and do their own jobs without interference from the boss. When your subordinates feel you trust them, they have more trust in you. Bradley even learned from Marshall that leaders should invite dissent so that they can have the widest range of options to choose from. Leaders are never well served by a staff of yes-men.

General Omar Bradley earned trust by walking around, talking to the troops, and being a good listener. His troops told him about problems with leadership, with equipment, and with morale. His troops would not have been so candid if they hadn't trusted him. Trust is crucial to keeping the lines of communication open. Trust can even be a force multiplier on the battlefield. To win your next battle, listen to your troops.

In June 2005, I went to Washington, DC, for the twenty-fifth anniversary celebration of the Washington Speakers Bureau. At the dessert table, I found myself reaching for the same chocolate éclair as General Colin Powell. I introduced myself and asked him if he had any leadership advice I could pass along to my son Bobby, who had just become a manager in minor league baseball. General Powell gave me several pieces of advice, but the most important advice he shared with me was this: "Tell your son, 'Take care of your troops.'"

That is the way Omar Bradley conducted his career. He took care of his troops, and they trusted him. If you take care of the people you lead, they will trust you and they will storm the beaches for you. General Bradley empowered his troops to believe they could accomplish anything, even the liberation of Europe.

They trusted him. He trusted them. And together, they got the job done.

Conclusion

HEROISM ON DISPLAY

Peter Wang, West Point class of 2025, was born in Brooklyn but spent his early childhood in China. His parents moved back to the United States when Peter was a preschooler and settled in Broward County, Florida, where they opened a Chinese restaurant. In the fall of 2017, fifteen-year-old Peter began his freshman year at Marjory Stoneman Douglas High School, where he was active in the Junior Reserve Officers' Training Corps (JROTC).

Fluent in English and Chinese, a top student, and a natural leader, Peter Wang had his heart set on attending the United States Military Academy at West Point. He had a lot to offer. According to his friends, he was a selfless and generous young man who was fun to be around. An avid fan of the Japanese anime art form, he enjoyed watching anime series such as *Dragon Ball Z* and *Naruto*.

On February 14, 2018, an angry and troubled nineteen-year-old former student of Marjory Stoneman Douglas High School walked onto the campus armed with an AR-15-style semiautomatic rifle and multiple ammo clips. The gunman set off a fire alarm to draw students out of their classrooms. When students appeared in the hallways, he opened fire.

When Wang heard the gunfire and realized what was happening, he opened a door to the outside and called to his fellow students to flee. Dressed in his JROTC uniform, Wang held the door open as students dashed to freedom. He was still holding the door when the gunman came around a corner and opened fire, killing him in cold blood.

Wang was one of seventeen people gunned down at the school that day. Just fifteen years old, he did the most noble and soldierly thing imaginable: while in uniform, he laid down his life for his friends.

The commander of his Bravo unit in JROTC, eighteen-year-old senior Angelyse Perez, remembered Wang as an excellent marksman and a dedicated cadet who was scheduled to be promoted in just one week. "That kid was the most hilarious thing on the planet," she said. "He was always happy and bubbly and smiley. . . . He was loved. That kid was loved."[1]

Chad Maxey, West Point class of 2004, heard about Wang's dream of attending West Point. He contacted the Academy, urging West Point to honor this fallen young hero. Maxey, an army veteran who served in both Iraq and Afghanistan, said, "It was clear from his classmates . . . that this was the type of person he was; they weren't surprised he would take this kind of action. He really did want to serve others."[2]

On Tuesday, February 20, Peter Wang was laid to rest with military honors. At the funeral, Captain Shain Uddin presented Wang's parents with a letter posthumously granting him admission to the West Point class of 2025. An Academy spokesman said, "Peter Wang, an Army Junior Reserve Officer Training Corps cadet at Marjory Stoneman Douglas High School, had a lifetime goal to attend USMA and was posthumously offered admission for his heroic actions on February 14, 2018. It was an appropriate way for USMA to honor this brave young man."[3]

Peter Wang exemplified the twelve West Point virtues—the twelve character traits commemorated in granite at Trophy Point:

compassion	integrity
courage	loyalty
dedication	perseverance
determination	responsibility
dignity	service
discipline	trust

In a single brave act, in the final defining moments of this young man's life, every one of those twelve character traits became starkly visible, etched into the soul of young Peter Wang. In spirit, in heroism, in virtue, he became part of that long gray line of West Point heroes.

His character was carved in stone.

Like all the others we have examined in these pages, this fifteen-year-old hero has set an example of character for us to follow. Whether you are in uniform or in civilian life, whether you have drilled and studied and trained on the West Point grounds or have never been within a thousand miles of the Academy, these are the character traits that will make you a leader, that will make you successful, that will enable you to live your life with honor.

And, perhaps, with heroism.

Notes

Introduction: The View from Trophy Point

1. James F. Finkenaur, "Robert G. Finkenaur 1934," WestPointAOG.org, http://apps.westpointaog.org/Memorials/Article/10024/.

2. Rick Atkinson, *The Long Gray Line: The American Journey of West Point's Class of 1966* (New York: Henry Holt & Co., 1989), 4.

3. Finkenaur, "Robert G. Finkenaur 1934."

4. James Charlton, *The Military Quotation Book: More than 1,200 of the Best Quotations about War, Leadership, Courage, Victory, and Defeat* (New York: St. Martin's Press, 2002), 83.

Chapter 1 Compassion: Warrior with a Heart

1. Ulysses S. Grant, *Personal Memoir of U. S. Grant, Volume I* (New York: Charles L. Webster & Co., 1885), 311.

2. Grant, *Personal Memoir of U. S. Grant*, 312.

3. Grant, *Personal Memoir of U. S. Grant*, 313.

4. American Battlefield Trust, "Ulysses S. Grant: The Myth of 'Unconditional Surrender' Begins at Fort Donelson," Battlefields.org, https://www.battlefields.org/learn/articles/ulysses-s-grant-myth-unconditional-surrender-begins-fort-donelson.

5. Bruce Catton, *U. S. Grant: The Civil War Years: Grant Moves South and Grant Takes Command* (New York: Open Road Media, 2016), Kindle edition.

6. Horace Porter, *Campaigning with Grant* (New York: Century, 1897), 515–16.

7. Porter, *Campaigning with Grant*, 164–65.

8. Porter, *Campaigning with Grant*, 63–64.

9. Porter, *Campaigning with Grant*, 102–3.

10. Alexander K. McClure, *Lincoln and Men of War-Times* (Philadelphia: Times Publishing Company, 1892), 195–96.

11. Frederick Douglass, *Life and Times of Frederick Douglass* (Boston: De Wolfe, Fiske, & Co., 1892), 434.

12. Ryan Tate, "What Everyone Is Too Polite to Say about Steve Jobs," Gawker .com, October 7, 2011, http://gawker.com/5847344/what-everyone-is-too-polite -to-say-about-steve-jobs.

13. Malcolm Gladwell, "The Tweaker: The Real Genius of Steve Jobs," *New Yorker*, November 14, 2011, http://www.newyorker.com/magazine/2011/11/14 /the-tweaker?currentPage=all.

14. Adam Lashinsky, "How Apple Works: Inside the World's Biggest Startup," *Fortune*, May 9, 2011, http://fortune.com/2011/05/09/how-apple-works-inside -the-worlds-biggest-startup/.

Chapter 2 Courage: Mastery over Fear

1. Bill Yenne, *Black '41: The West Point Class of 1941 and the American Triumph in WWII* (Hoboken, NJ: John Wiley & Sons, 1991), 81.

2. Franklin Mering Reck, *Beyond the Call of Duty* (New York: Thomas Y. Crowell Co., 1944), 2.

3. Alexander Nininger Sr., "Alexander R. Nininger, Jr. 1941," WestPointAOG .org, accessed January 29, 2018, http://apps.westpointaog.org/Memorials/Article /12317/.

4. Nininger, "Alexander R. Nininger, Jr. 1941."

5. USMA Office of Chaplains, "Cadet Prayer," USMA.edu, https://www.usma .edu/chaplain/sitepages/cadet%20prayer.aspx.

6. Justin Moore, "Leading from the Front Lines," *Fast Company*, May 30, 2012, https://www.fastcompany.com/1838811/leading-front-lines.

7. Colonel Robert J. Dalessandro, *Army Officer's Guide*, 51st Edition (Mechanicsburg, PA: Stackpole Books, 2009), vii, xi.

Chapter 3 Dedication: What Heroes Are Made Of

1. Rod Pyle, "Apollo 11's Scariest Moments: Perils of the 1st Manned Moon Landing," Space.com, July 21, 2014, https://www.space.com/26593-apollo-11 -moon-landing-scariest-moments.html.

2. Ben Evans, *Foothold in the Heavens: The Seventies* (New York: Springer, 2010), 298.

3. Ben Cosgrove, "America's First Space Walk: Edward White Makes History, June 1965," *Time*, October 1, 2013, http://time.com/3739536/americas-first-space -walk-edward-white-makes-history-june-1965/.

4. Buzz Aldrin with Ken Abraham, *No Dream Is Too High: Life Lessons from a Man Who Walked on the Moon* (Washington, DC: National Geographic, 2016), 53.

5. Edgar Albert Guest, originally published in the *Detroit Free Press*, from the *Cambrian* 34, no. 5 (March 1, 1919): 16 (public domain).

6. Robin McKie, "How Michael Collins Became the Forgotten Astronaut of Apollo 11," *The Guardian*, July 18, 2009, https://www.theguardian.com/science /2009/jul/19/michael-collins-astronaut-apollo11.

7. McKie, "Forgotten Astronaut of Apollo 11."

8. McKie, "Forgotten Astronaut of Apollo 11."
9. McKie, "Forgotten Astronaut of Apollo 11."
10. Michael Collins, *Carrying the Fire: An Astronaut's Journey* (New York: Cooper Square Press, 2001), 451–52.
11. Frank Borman (interviewed by David Siry), "An Astronaut Examines the Honor System at West Point," West Point Center for Oral History, October 19, 2016, video transcribed by the authors, http://www.westpointcoh.org/interviews/an-astronaut-examines-the-honor-system-at-west-point.
12. Borman, "An Astronaut Examines the Honor System."
13. Borman, "An Astronaut Examines the Honor System."
14. Meg Jones (*Milwaukee Journal Sentinel*), "Apollo Astronaut Frank Borman Remembers the View," Phys.org, October 7, 2016, https://phys.org/news/2016-10-apollo-astronaut-frank-borman-view.html.
15. Robert Kurson, *Rocket Men: The Daring Odyssey of Apollo 8 and the Astronauts Who Made Man's First Journey to the Moon* (New York: Random House, 2018), 262.
16. E. B. Boyd, "Popvox CEO Marci Harris on Assembling a Dedicated Team with a Shared Vision," *Fast Company*, November 26, 2012, https://www.fastcompany.com/3003117/popvox-ceo-marci-harris-assembling-dedicated-team-shared-vision.

Chapter 4 Determination: Never Give Up

1. Ira Berkow, "West Point Is Standing at Attention for Army Women's Coach," *New York Times*, March 15, 2006, https://www.nytimes.com/2006/03/15/sports/sportsspecial1/west-point-is-standing-at-attention-for-army-womens.html.
2. Elizabeth Merrill, "Maggie Dixon Still Revered for Her Impact," ESPN.com, April 8, 2011, http://www.espn.com/ncw/news/story?id=6289706 (dialogue based on Coach Doug Bruno's narrative account).
3. Merrill, "Maggie Dixon Still Revered."
4. Diane H. Mazur, *A More Perfect Military: How the Constitution Can Make Our Military Stronger* (New York: Oxford University Press, 2010), 165–66.
5. General H. Norman Schwarzkopf, interview by Brian Lamb, "It Doesn't Take a Hero," Booknotes.org (C-Span), program air date November 22, 1992, transcript http://www.booknotes.org/Watch/35014-1/Gen-Norman-Schwarzkopf.
6. Norman Schwarzkopf, *It Doesn't Take a Hero: The Autobiography of General Norman Schwarzkopf* (New York: Bantam, 1992), 198.

Chapter 5 Dignity: Every Inch a Soldier

1. Frank Everson Vandiver, *Black Jack: The Life and Times of John J. Pershing*, vol. 1 (College Station: Texas A&M University Press, 1977), 32.
2. Vandiver, *Black Jack*, 33.
3. John J. Pershing, *My Life before the World War, 1860–1917: A Memoir* (Lexington: University Press of Kentucky, 2013), 45.
4. Vandiver, *Black Jack*, 127.
5. Cora W. Rowell, *Leaders of the Great War* (New York: Macmillan, 1920), 265.
6. Rowell, *Leaders of the Great War*, 265–66.

7. Pershing, *My Life before the World War*, 285.

8. Pershing, *My Life before the World War*, 284–85.

9. Daniel Immerwahr, "One Record of General Pershing's Quite Cordial Relationship with Filipino Muslims," *Slate*, August 18, 2017, http://www.slate.com/blogs/the_vault/2017/08/18/how_general_john_pershing_actually_dealt_with_filipino_muslims.html.

10. Pershing, *My Life before the World War*, 192–93.

11. Immerwahr, "General Pershing's Quite Cordial Relationship."

12. Michael Keane, *George S. Patton: Blood, Guts, and Prayer* (Washington, DC: Regnery, 2014), 116.

13. Kate Louise Roberts, *Hoyt's New Cyclopedia of Practical Quotations* (New York: Funk & Wagnalls, 1923), 194.

14. Carrie Kerpen, "You Must Always Treat People with Dignity," *Forbes*, January 29, 2018, https://www.forbes.com/sites/carriekerpen/2018/01/29/you-must-always-treat-people-with-dignity/.

15. Bud Bilanich, "Treat Everyone You Meet with Dignity and Respect," *Fast Company*, August 12, 2008, https://www.fastcompany.com/958644/treat-everyone-you-meet-dignity-and-respect.

Chapter 6 Discipline: Excellence Is a Habit

1. Stephen E. Ambrose, *Duty, Honor, Country: A History of West Point* (Baltimore: Johns Hopkins University Press, 1999), 66–67.

2. Wilson Miles, Cary Fairfax, Thomas Ragland, and Nathaniel Hall Loring, *An Expose of Facts Concerning Recent Transactions Relating to the Corps of Cadets of the United States Military Academy at West Point, New York* (Newburgh, NY: Uriah C. Lewis, 1819), 67.

3. Dwight Thomas and David Kelly Jackson, eds., *The Poe Log: A Documentary Life of Edgar Allan Poe, 1809-1849* (Boston: G. K. Hall & Co., 1987), 107–18; J. Gerald Kennedy, ed., *A Historical Guide to Edgar Allan Poe* (New York: Oxford University Press, 2001), 28–29.

4. Will Durant, *The Story of Philosophy* (New York: Pocket Books, 2006), 98.

5. Harry S. Truman, "Longhand Note of Judge Harry S. Truman, May 14, 1934," Harry S. Truman Presidential Library & Museum, https://www.trumanlibrary.org/whistlestop/study_collections/trumanpapers/psf/longhand/index.php?documentid=hst-psf_naid735210-01.

Chapter 7 Integrity: Honest and True

1. Stephen E. Ambrose, *Eisenhower: Soldier, General of the Army, President-Elect, 1890-1952* (New York: Simon & Schuster, 1983), 153.

2. Alan Axelrod, *Eisenhower on Leadership: Ike's Enduring Lessons in Total Victory Management* (San Francisco: Jossey-Bass, 2006), 40.

3. Axelrod, *Eisenhower on Leadership*, 40–41.

4. Joseph A. Maciariello, *A Year with Peter Drucker: 52 Weeks of Coaching for Leadership Effectiveness* (New York: HarperCollins, 2014), 6.

5. William B. Mead and Paul Dickson, *Baseball: The Presidents' Game* (New York: Walker & Co., 1997), 95.

6. Stephen E. Ambrose, *Eisenhower: Soldier and President* (New York: Simon & Schuster, 1990), 16–17.

7. Dwight D. Eisenhower, *At Ease: Stories I Tell to Friends* (Garden City, NY: Doubleday, 1967), 39.

8. Mead and Dickson, *Baseball*, 93.

9. Ambrose, *Eisenhower: Soldier and President*, 44.

10. Stanley Weintraub, *15 Stars: Eisenhower, MacArthur, Marshall—Three Generals Who Saved the American Century* (New York: Free Press, 2007), xvi.

11. Matthew F. Holland, *Eisenhower between the Wars: The Making of a General and Statesman* (Westport, CT: Greenwood, 2001), 188.

12. Weintraub, *15 Stars*, xii.

13. Ambrose, *Eisenhower: Soldier and President*, 54.

14. Charles J. Pellerin, *How NASA Builds Teams: Mission Critical Soft Skills for Scientists, Engineers, and Project Teams* (Hoboken, NJ: Wiley, 2009), 77.

15. Carlo D'Este, *Eisenhower: A Soldier's Life* (New York: Henry Holt, 2002), 526.

16. Stephen E. Ambrose, *D-Day, June 6, 1944: The Climactic Battle of World War II* (New York: Simon & Schuster, 1994), 171.

17. D'Este, *Eisenhower: A Soldier's Life*, 527.

18. Ambrose, *D-Day*, 329.

19. D'Este, *Eisenhower: A Soldier's Life*, 527.

20. Weintraub, *15 Stars*, 392.

21. Robert A. Wilson, *Character above All: Ten Presidents from FDR to George Bush* (New York: Simon & Schuster, 1995), 63.

22. John W. Malsberger, *The General and the Politician: Dwight Eisenhower, Richard Nixon, and American Politics* (Lanham, MD: Rowman & Littlefield, 2014), xi.

23. Malsberger, *The General and the Politician*, 191.

24. Malsberger, *The General and the Politician*, 3.

25. David Haven Blake, *Liking Ike: Eisenhower, Advertising, and the Rise of Celebrity Politics* (New York: Oxford University Press, 2016), 73.

26. Carlo D'Este, "The Myth of Ike and Kay Summersby Part IV—Conclusion," ArmchairGeneral.com, August 4, 2013, http://armchairgeneral.com/the-myth-of-ike-and-kay-summersby-part-iv-conclusion.htm.

27. Michael E. Haskew, *West Point 1915: Eisenhower, Bradley, and the Class the Stars Fell On* (Minneapolis: Zenith Press, 2014), 57.

Chapter 8 Loyalty: He Knew Their Names

1. George Charles Mitchell, *Matthew B. Ridgway: Soldier, Statesman, Scholar, Citizen* (Mechanicsburg, PA: Stackpole Books, 2002), 10.

2. Matthew B. Ridgway with Harold H. Martin, *Soldier: The Memoirs of Matthew B. Ridgway* (New York: Harper & Brothers, 1956), 97–98.

3. Carlo D'Este, "Ridgway: Iron Man at the Front," History.com, March 4, 2013, http://www.historynet.com/ridgway-iron-man-at-the-front.htm.

4. Ridgway with Martin, *Soldier*, 2.

5. Ridgway with Martin, *Soldier*, 103.

6. Ridgway with Martin, *Soldier*, 102–3.

7. Max Hastings, *Armageddon: The Battle for Germany, 1944–45* (New York: Vintage, 2004), 225.

8. George Charles Mitchell, *Matthew B. Ridgway: Soldier, Statesman, Scholar, Citizen* (Mechanicsburg, PA: Stackpole Books, 2002), back cover.

9. Donald J. Farinacci, *Truman and MacArthur: Adversaries for a Common Cause* (Hoosick Falls, NY: Merriam Press, 2017), 260.

10. United States Army, "The Army Values," accessed February 12, 2018, https://www.army.mil/values/.

Chapter 9 Perseverance: Refuse to Quit

1. Cadet Alexandra Efaw, "Band of Sisters—West Point Is in Their DNA," United States Army, October 28, 2013, https://www.army.mil/article/113980/band_of_sisters_west_point_is_in_their_dna.

2. Kevin Cahillane, Rumsey Taylor, Josh Williams, and Margaret Cheatham Williams, "The Women of West Point," *New York Times*, September 4, 2014, http://www.nytimes.com/interactive/2014/09/04/magazine/women-of-west-point.html?_r=0.

3. Cahillane et al., "The Women of West Point."

4. Cahillane et al., "The Women of West Point."

5. Rona Marech, "Army Officer, 23, Leapt High in Life Cut Short by War," *Baltimore Sun*, September 22, 2006, http://www.baltimoresun.com/news/maryland/bal-md.perez22sep-story.html.

6. Joshua Garner, "Family Keeps County Soldier's Memory Alive," the *Gazette* (Maryland), February 26, 2009, http://www.gazette.net/stories/02262009/uppenew171724_32475.shtml.

7. Captain Walter Bryan Jackson, "Nininger Award Acceptance Speech," USMA, September 17, 2008, https://www.westpointaog.org/document.doc?id=1083.

8. This version of the Robert Strauss maxim has been quoted by John Maxwell and others. Strauss's actual wording, which I prefer not to quote, is a bit earthier and can be found in Kathryn J. McGarr, *The Whole Damn Deal: Robert Strauss and the Art of Politics* (New York: Public Affairs, 2011), 131.

9. Vincent van Gogh, "Letter from Vincent van Gogh to Theo van Gogh, Drenthe, 28 October 1883," Webexhibits.org, http://www.webexhibits.org/vangogh/letter/13/336.htm, emphasis in the original.

Chapter 10 Responsibility: "No Excuse, Sir!"

1. Mike Krzyzewski with Donald T. Phillips, *Leading with the Heart: Coach K's Successful Strategies for Basketball, Business, and Life* (New York: Warner, 2000), 42.

2. Krzyzewski with Phillips, *Leading with the Heart*, 40–45.

3. Douglas MacArthur, *Reminiscences* (Annapolis, MD: Naval Institute Press, 1964, 2001), 140.

4. Christopher L. Kolakowski, *Last Stand on Bataan: The Defense of the Philippines, December 1941–May 1942* (Jefferson, NC: McFarland & Co., 2016), 137.

5. Arthur Herman, *Douglas MacArthur: American Warrior* (New York: Random House, 2017), 404.

6. Herman, *Douglas MacArthur: American Warrior*, 411.

7. Frazier Hunt, *MacArthur and the War against Japan* (New York: Charles Scribner's Sons, 1944), 71.

8. Bernard K. Duffy and Ronald H. Carpenter, *Douglas MacArthur: Warrior as Wordsmith* (Westport, CT: Greenwood Press, 1997), 17.

9. Suzanne McIntire, *American Heritage Book of Great American Speeches for Young People* (New York: John Wiley & Sons, 2001), 171–72.

Chapter 11 Service: Humble and Selfless

1. Laurence M. Hauptman and Heriberto Dixon, "From West Point to Wahoo Swamp: The Career of Cadet David Moniac, Class of 1822," *American Indian*, Spring 2016, http://www.americanindianmagazine.org/story/west-point-wahoo -swamp?page=show.

2. Hauptman and Dixon, "West Point to Wahoo Swamp."

3. Documents, Legislative and Executive, of the Congress of the United States, *American State Papers, Class V, Military Affairs*, vol. 2 (Washington, DC: Gales and Seaton, 1834), 13.

4. CSM Dan Elder, USA (Ret.), *NCO Guide: 10th Edition* (Mechanicsburg, PA: Stackpole, 2015), 51.

5. Command Sgt. Maj. Brunk W. Conley, "What the Warrior Ethos Means to Me," Army University Press, NCO Journal, February 2018, https://www.armyu press.army.mil/Journals/NCO-Journal/Archives/2018/February/Warrior-Ethos/.

Chapter 12 Trust: The GI's General

1. Jim DeFelice, *Omar Bradley: General at War* (Washington, DC: Regnery, 2011), 17.

2. Omar Nelson Bradley, *A Soldier's Story* (New York: Modern Library, 1999), xvi.

3. Michael E. Haskew, *West Point 1915: Eisenhower, Bradley, and the Class the Stars Fell On* (Minneapolis: Zenith Press, 2014), 42.

4. DeFelice, *Omar Bradley*, 40.

5. DeFelice, *Omar Bradley*, 42.

6. DeFelice, *Omar Bradley*, 140.

7. DeFelice, *Omar Bradley*, 3–4.

8. Richard C. Gross, "General of the Armies Omar Bradley was buried on . . . ," UPI Archives, April 14, 1981, https://www.upi.com/Archives/1981/04/14/General -of-the-Armies-Omar-Bradley-was-buried-on/2827356072400/.

9. Steven L. Ossad, *Omar Nelson Bradley: America's GI General* (Columbia, MO: University of Missouri Press, 2017), 328.

10. Todd Bermont, *Cognitive Selling: Proven Fundamentals & Techniques of the World's Most Effective Sales People* (Chicago: 10 Step, 2004), 139.

11. DeFelice, *Omar Bradley*, 4.

12. Edgar F. Puryear Jr., *Nineteen Stars: A Study in Military Character and Leadership* (Novato, CA: Presidio Press, 1981), 290.

13. DeFelice, *Omar Bradley*, 50.

Conclusion: Heroism on Display

1. Alex Harris, "Peter Wang, Who Died a 'Hero' in the Parkland Shooting, Remembered as Brave and Funny," *Miami Herald*, February 19, 2018, http://www.miamiherald.com/news/local/community/broward/article200992699.html.

2. Susan Svrluga, "'Heroic': West Point Admits a Student Who Was Killed in the Parkland Shooting," *Washington Post*, February 20, 2018, https://www.washingtonpost.com/news/grade-point/wp/2018/02/20/heroic-west-point-admits-a-student-who-was-killed-in-the-parkland-shooting/.

3. Svrluga, "'Heroic.'"

Pat Williams is senior vice president of the NBA's Orlando Magic. He has more than 50 years of professional sports experience; has written more than 100 books, including the popular *Coach Wooden, The Difference You Make*, and *The Sweet Spot for Success*; and is one of America's most sought-after motivational speakers. He lives in Florida. Find out more at www.patwilliams.com.

Jim Denney is the author of *Walt's Disneyland, Answers to Satisfy the Soul, Writing in Overdrive*, and the Timebenders series for young readers. He has written many books with Pat Williams, including *Coach Wooden, The Difference You Make*, and *The Sweet Spot for Success*. Learn more at www.writinginoverdrive.com.

CONNECT WITH PAT

We would love to hear from you. Please send your comments about this book to Pat Williams:

pwilliams@orlandomagic.com

Pat Williams
c/o Orlando Magic
8701 Maitland Summit Boulevard
Orlando, FL 32810

If you would like to set up a speaking engagement for Pat, please contact his assistant, Andrew Herdliska:
(407) 916-2401
aherdliska@orlandomagic.com

PATWILLIAMS.COM

 OrlandoMagicPatWilliams

 OrlandoMagicPat

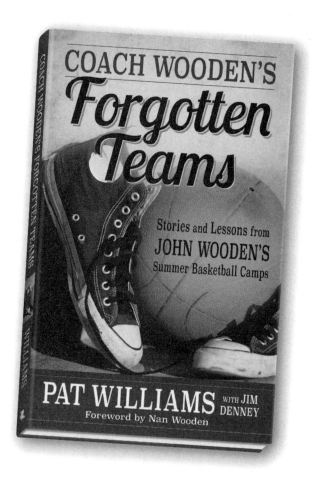

Inspiration and Guidance for a Life of
INTEGRITY and EXCELLENCE

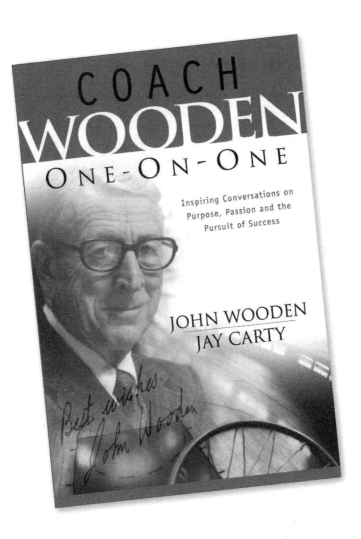

Coach Wooden Knew the Long-Term Impact of
LITTLE THINGS DONE WELL

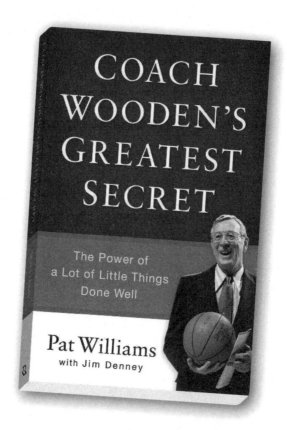

A motivational message filled with life-changing insights and memorable stories—Pat Williams shares why the secret to success in life depends on a lot of little things done well.

FIND SUCCESS WHERE YOUR
TALENT AND PASSIONS MEET

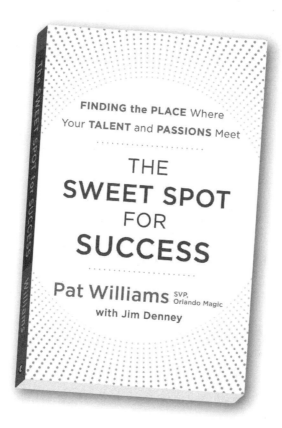

FINDING the PLACE Where
Your TALENT and PASSIONS Meet

THE
SWEET SPOT
FOR
SUCCESS

Pat Williams SVP, Orlando Magic
with Jim Denney

The SWEET SPOT for SUCCESS

Williams

"Pat Williams's waste-no-time philosophy has informed my work ethic for decades. *The Sweet Spot for Success* distills all he's learned and put into practice. Pat lays it out in such a way that you can easily intersect your talent with your passion to discover your sweet spot in life. Now *that's* success!"

—JERRY B. JENKINS, novelist and biographer;
founder, The Jerry Jenkins Writers Guild